Acknowledgements

I would like to thank all the artists, gallery directors, exhibition organisers and others who willingly gave their time in interviews and through questionnaires. Special thanks to Paul Bonaventura, David Butler, Richard Ducker, Diana Irving, Malcolm Miles, Maureen Paley, Helen Smith and Anne Wallace for their ideas, practical help, support and faith in the project.

About the author

Debbie Duffin is an artist who has shown widely in London, the regions and France, with work represented in private and public collections. She began her career organising her own exhibitions, which led to offers of shows in a range of galleries and exhibition spaces and to her collaborating on artist led events. At the same time she began to be invited to work for commercial and funded galleries as a freelance organiser/ consultant. Her own struggles to come to terms with life as a professional artist have led to the development of innovative workshops for artists and students, exploring the complex issues facing artists today. Her first book, *Organising Your Exhibition*, provided much needed practical advice on exhibition organising, which she herself had lacked. Her commitment to the empowerment of artists continues through this second publication and an on-going involvement with education and training for artists.

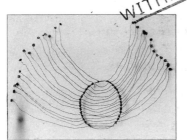

Wire piece,
Debbie Duffin,
18"x13' 1994

3

Contents

Forword 6

Introduction 7

1 • The art world 8
Artists attitudes & definitions 8, Artists as stars 9, Dealers & gallerists 10, Curators & organisers 10, Collectors 11, Press & media 13, Art market 15, Motivations & agendas 16, Hierarchies & careers 17, Changes & developments 19, Politics & economics 19, Gender 20, Cultural diversity 21, Age 22, Shifting centres 23

2 • Galleries & exhibition spaces 25
Commercial galleries 25, Subsidised galleries 32, Artist-run spaces 39, Spaces in other contexts 43, Hire galleries 47

3 • Temporary presentations 49

4 • Open exhibitions 54

5 • Independent curators 58

6 • Sales commission 61

7 • Education & interpretation 63

8 • Self-assessment 66
Strategy 67, Research 69, Making an informed choice 70, Creating opportunities 71, Action plan 72

9 • Approaching galleries 78
Telephone techniques 78, Making applications 79, Interviews & studio visits 85

Contents

10 • Making an exhibition work 88
Promotion 89, The show is up 90, What if things go wrong 92, Selling work 93, Documentation 94, Assessing your work 95, Broadening audiences 96

11 • Evaluating the experience 100
Starting work again 101, Continuing gallery relationships 101, What next? 102, Developing a context 103, Success 104, Making choices 106

12 • Further reading 107

13 • Contacts 110

14 • Index 112

Foreword

Lubaina Himid
Artist, curator, teacher and Senior Lecturer in Fine Art, University of Central Lancashire.

At last, a book that encourages daring, discourages bitterness and seriously could empower.

It is important to realise that much of the art world functions as it does, that is to say mysteriously, because of the enormous variety of hidden agendas, ranging from private incomes to career curators and poor art school teaching to fear of the unknown. In this book, Debbie Duffin offers excellent and realistic analysis which clears up much of the muddle. By looking at the system as a whole, she attempts to prepare artists for the challenge of sharing their vision with the world in a positive and energetic way.

Being an artist can be a struggle. Keeping going is really half of the battle. Artists must combine action with experience. They must be aware of what is going on around them locally as well as nationally and internationally whilst at the same time being true to their own ideals. As knowing how and where to place art work – bearing in mind ambition and dividing it by ability, time, money and energy – is a difficult lesson to learn, the information articulated here is vital: it will encourage artists to evaluate situations and locations for themselves.

Artists will find all sort of puzzling anomalies revealed in this book and even a seasoned practitioner in need of a plan of action will discover something useful. This is both a guide and a friendly reminder of how things are.

Debbie Duffin's generosity in sharing her research is a brave and positive move which should be applauded and rewarded. It should encourage all of us to share our knowledge, our hard-won information and our skills as well as our successes.

Introduction

See also 'Commercial galleries', Debbie Duffin, *Artists Newsletter*, June, 1990

"The creative process is only complete when the work has been seen." That exhibiting is vitally important to artists is an opinion endorsed by Albert Irvin in the comment above, and one shared by many others. My experience as an artist shows that having a realistic attitude to approaching galleries and the art world, clearly identifying aims and ambitions and acquiring confidence to work towards them, gaining necessary skills and recognising the flexibility, commitment and work involved and being prepared for the results of success are essential ingredients for artists planning to develop their careers through exhibiting.

In *Organising Your Exhibition,* I addressed some of these issues by encouraging artists to take control of their careers and organise exhibitions themselves. In this book, I explore the broader issues of developing an exhibiting career, looking at the nature of the art world, the range and scope of galleries and exhibition spaces, and exploring the practicalities of the exhibition process.

Throughout the book, comments and advice from artists and others are interwoven with practical information and analysis. The book can therefore be read from start to finish, sections picked out according to a particular need, or alternatively, as a source of information, ideas and advice, it can be 'dipped into' again and again.

Artists discover many ways of developing their careers. Aspirations vary and methods of achieving ambitions can be unpredictable as well as exciting. By dealing with the choices and decisions which artists have to make along the way, this book makes a valuable contribution to demystifying a complex situation. For whilst artists may seem to begin from a position of disadvantage this can change. As artists, we can harness our energy, enthusiasm, skills, talents and ideas to empower ourselves. By seeking equal relationships with others, we can take a more positive role in the development of contemporary visual arts practices, particularly the world of exhibitions, whilst at the same time carving out individual career paths for ourselves.

1 • The art world

Whilst some artists thoroughly enjoy their careers, seizing opportunities, fulfilling themselves and their ambitions and finding the art world a challenge, this isn't always the case. Others may not begin to achieve what they want, perhaps feeling forced to choose between integrity and success, or blaming the art world for lack of recognition. They may not even want to be considered part of a system in which they feel used and manipulated.

However, deciding to become an artist means accepting you are part of the art world. By taking an art qualification, putting a mark on the page, looking at work in galleries and elsewhere, artists are staking their claim in it. There may be uncomfortable features, conditions in need of change, but no artist is outside it. Whether claiming to be 'mainstream', 'alternative', 'inside' or 'outside', artists, galleries, exhibitions and critics are interrelated and mutually dependent.

Artists' attitudes & definitions

From British American Arts Association conference publication *Artist in the Changing City*, 1993

"The definition of the term 'artist' varies widely .... Nationality, ethnicity, class, wealth and culture all influence the concept of artist." Artists who took part in the 'Artist in the Changing City' conference gave widely divergent definitions of themselves and their activities. One said he saw himself as scavenging a living on the fringe of society. Artist and film-maker Peter Sellars sees artists are communicators "that's why they are at the centre of this society." Whilst some artists, dissatisfied with the lack of or nature of opportunities available, take on the role of organiser, curator and entrepreneur, others dismiss this, feeling the artist's only concern is making.

The range of media, content, concerns and forms is growing and although some artists use the traditional forms of painting and sculpture, others experiment with video, film and live art. Abstract, conceptual and issue-based work may be articulated through paint, print, film or computer generated imagery. Some works combine media – sculptural forms with video and performance with drawing materials. Work may be made to last or be ephemeral. Context and collaboration with other professionals has also had an impact as artists have emerged from the studio and confronted the needs of others.

Differing ambitions, approaches and concerns lead to different career patterns. Cornelia Parker's reputation grew through showing in public galleries and Kevin Atherton's through the siting of work in public places. Simon Edmondson's work has largely been shown through commercial galleries and he makes a living from selling. Albert Irvin taught for many years and was only taken on by Gimpel Fils in his 60s.

Artists as stars

Many artists embrace the concept that they should strive to become 'stars', believing that if they are 'good' enough or lucky enough, they could be the next 'big name'. But a tiny minority achieve this and for some, it is a short-lived role. The path to stardom is accompanied by heightened media attention, an increased number of sales at successively higher prices and a number of firm promises of exhibitions. The work itself becomes the subject of vigorous debate, and a 'star' is under pressure to take part in activities which promote them as a personality too.

The Conditions of Success, Alan Bowness, Thames & Hudson, 1989

Rise to stardom is not necessarily age-related. Although some gain it whilst young, others find stardom after many years of hard and consistent work. Alan Bowness has identified four "circles of recognition: ... peer recognition, critical recognition, patronage by dealers and collectors and finally public acclaim." The nature of the work must strike a chord in others, perhaps 'mirroring' the state of the times. It usually involves co-operation between artist and others: agents, galleries and/or the media, all of whom have a vested interest.

Relative Values, Louisa Buck & Philip Dodd, BBC, 1991

The successful 'stars' are perhaps those who willingly collaborate. "With so much attention paid to the artist, and with the marketability of his status, it is small wonder that certain artists have taken the actual image of 'the Artist' and sold it like a commodity." Some successful artists energetically pursue self-promotion, putting acclaim before anything else. Subsequently, they have been labelled egotistical and demanding by galleries and other exhibitors.

Nevertheless, most work hard to gain 'stardom' and possess a degree of toughness and stamina others might find hard to maintain.

Dealers & gallerists

People who buy and sell art from galleries, auction houses and from artists themselves are called dealers. Although many dealers also run galleries as the public face of their business and a showcase for their artists, not all commercial gallery directors are dealers. Dealers are considered to have a high degree of control over the art market and what sells, to whom and for how much. However, they will argue that it is auction houses which shape demand for art and the prices for which it is sold. 'Gallerists' is a relatively new term used here and abroad to describe people who run galleries but who are not dealers.

Curators & organisers

See also **5 •**
Independent
curators Curator, a term originally used for those responsible for permanent collections in museums, nowadays describes those who conceive exhibitions, make aesthetic decisions about content and take artistic responsibility for a one-off exhibition, installation or an entire exhibition programme. Curators tend to be held in higher regard than administrators or exhibition organisers who are viewed as people who deal predominantly with the practical side of organising exhibitions. However, in practice, there is a blurring of these two roles and interpretation depends largely on the skills and experience of individual curators and organisers.

Curators may be employed by galleries and museums or may work on a freelance basis, collaborating with a number of galleries and/or setting up their own events which provide freedom to develop their ideas. Many others – including academics, critics, writers and artists – occasionally act as curators.

Well-respected curators and the shows they put together can greatly enhance artists' careers. Many work with a relatively small but perhaps changing group of artists to whose work they relate, and with whom the curator feels s/he can realise an ambition. However, the trend towards curators developing concepts and defining frameworks for shows has led some artists to feel their independence is being compromised by the need to contextualise their work.

Collectors

Selling the Contemporary Visual Arts, Gerri Morris, Arts Council, 1992

Private collectors range from people who occasionally buy a modestly-priced art work to hang on the wall at home to those with international reputations who may love the work they buy, but also consider art acquisition in terms of investment and status. The typical buyer of contemporary art, as defined by some recent research, is someone who works in the creative, caring or media professions, has been educated to degree level and who has unconventional attitudes and a desire to be a 'fashion leader'. As would be expected, many people working in the visual arts world collect work and this includes gallery directors who may buy work they exhibit.

People who collect with status, investment or glory in mind, necessarily have a vested interest in contributing to the marketing of artists whose work they own, and have their part to play in the promotion of artist and art work. Having work collected can enhance an artist's reputation by encouraging others to show, buy and promote their work.

Whilst some collectors rely on their own knowledge and business sense and develop an eye for new talent, others prefer to be guided by galleries. Some build a reputation for collecting a particular type of work, whereas others adjust collections as their interests change and they grow more knowledgeable about visual arts.

Corporate collections

Business collections may start off quite simply with occasional purchases of small pieces for offices and boardrooms. Companies who take a more co-ordinated approach sometimes employ a gallery or agent to work with them on developing the collection. An example of this is Art for Offices who offers this service to corporate customers. But as buying or commissioning art works is recognised as an important way of enhancing the corporate image it follows that if a company wants to gain a high-profile it may have to purchase work by high-profile artists with prices to match.

The Functions and Benefits of Corporate Art, unpublished research in 1988 by T Gertik showing that 450 companies had corporate collections is referred to *Public Art in Private Places*, Roberts, March and Salter, University of Westminster, 1993 as demonstrating potential markets for public art.

Though collections may be organised by the person in a company most interested in art, selection of work is often made by a staff group, sometimes with guidance from an 'art expert' and financial advisor.

Public collections

Having work included in a major museum collection is a significant achievement for an artist which helps create an historical context for the work and by doing so, contributes to its accessibility, acceptance

View of the refurbished Cleveland Crafts Centre, Middlesbrough showing the collection.
Collections of studio pottery and international non-precious jewellery are shown in a large open room in what is intended as a deliberately relaxed environment. As the result of an active acquisitions policy, the pottery collection has doubled in size in five years, the centre's view being that "Collections which don't grow are stranded in time and place, the contents having no reference to past or future." The collection adds to the centre's credibility and has encouraged some better-known makers to participate in the programme of changing exhibitions.

and value. Public collections include those held by local authority museums which in the past were important collectors of contemporary art. However, as acquisition funds have largely been cut, nowadays purchases of contemporary art can generally only be made when assisted by V&A or Contemporary Art Society purchase funds or when Friends Scheme funds are available.

Local authority libraries and other organisations sometimes run picture loan schemes in which small-scale work is hired out at low charges to people to hang in their homes. Works usually come from local amateur and professional artists and is selected to appeal to local tastes.

The Arts Council of England's collection of contemporary art includes work of established and lesser-known artists. Purchases are made by a changing panel drawn from the gallery world, who select through studio and gallery visits. As works in the collection are regularly loaned out for exhibition, there is an obvious benefit to artists represented. The British Council also collects work, used to promote British art and artists abroad through exhibitions and other events.

Art works also play an important part in creating pleasant surroundings in healthcare settings. Improving the visual environment has been proved as helpful in

The Scottish Arts Council has now put 2200 works from its collection on an interactive computer system. Eventually, images will be accessible in schools and libraries around Scotland either on-line or through CD-ROM. The Crafts Council's collection is included in their "interactive picture bank of 35,000 images" launched in May 1994 and which can be accessed in their London-based offices. Users can take away print-outs of selected images or order slides for a "modest fee".

The gallery at Aberdeen Royal Infirmary.

Programmed by Grampian Hospitals Art Project, this gallery shows work by local artists throughout the year. Commission from sale of work buys work to add to the project's collection of over 800 art works by contemporary Scottish artists which are on continuous display in Aberdeen hospitals. As well as developing the collection, the project's on-going commissions programme initiates projects which enable sculpture, murals, prints, installations and craft work to be sited in Grampian Hospitals.

improving recovery rates, and an increasing number of hospitals, health centres and clinics are purchasing and commissioning works of art.

Press & media

Media coverage can play an important part in a gallery's success and development of an artist's career. A review tends to give the work status and may lead to increased visitors and sales. It may also attract the attention of collectors and other galleries. Media coverage, especially if on network television, has the effect of increasing an artist's public profile and may subsequently contribute to an increase in the work's value as well as to more opportunities for the artist to show and sell.

Periodicals and programmes must, however, be concerned with satisfying and maintaining audiences. For example, a local radio programme or newspaper will tend to report on the 'human' angle of an artist's exhibition, pitching what it says to appeal to a broad cross-section of the public. Specialist art and craft magazines are more concerned with the content, 'quality' and contemporary context. Each develops its own editorial criteria: *Art Monthly* leans towards reviewing issue-based work; *Contemporary Art* takes a more traditional approach to reviewing painting and sculpture exhibitions; *Crafts* magazine looks critically at the fine art end of contemporary craft and *Circa* reviews "contemporary visual culture in Ireland".

Writers & critics

How visual arts is presented in the art press depends largely on the interest of particular writers or critics and the editorial stance of the publications to which they contribute. Policies may quickly change if a new editor is appointed.

Freelance writers may seem to have more freedom than employed writers to sell articles to a variety of publications, but there is no guarantee anything they offer will be published. Inevitably, publishers receive far more submissions than space allows. Some freelancers develop relationships with employers which provide scope for personal development. Sarah Kent, visual arts editor of *Time Out*, chooses exhibition reviewers from a pool of freelancers, selecting "the person most likely to relate to the exhibition." Art magazines like *Art Monthly* combine using regular contributors with commissioning new writers if their style and interests match the magazine's. The support of a writer or critic can greatly advance the development of an artist's career and an ambitious artist must court attention from reviewers.

The BBC 2 programme '40 Minutes', produced by the Community Education Unit, was planning a programme on arts in the North East. Researchers telephoned some visual arts organisations including an artists' studio group. The group sent a recent exhibition catalogue which had emphasised the role artists played in the community. Producer and film crew spent two days in the region following up leads. As a result, half the programme described a project being undertaken by one artist in the group.

Researchers

Television arts and media programmes invariably use researchers to provide background information and contacts on a particular topic for programme producers and editors. They do most of their work by telephone and often to tight deadlines. Visual material is generally only asked for at 'short-list' stage.

Editorial decisions

There is an overwhelming choice of exhibitions and related events to cover. Press and media people receive hundreds of invitations and press releases as well as many personal approaches from artists, galleries and arts organisers. For *Art Monthly* editor Patricia Bickers, factors which influence her decision about what to review include whether the show fits the editorial style and maintains balance between short reviews and in-depth critiques and between regional and London shows. As only ten issues are published annually and deadlines are at least a month before publication, a show wouldn't be reviewed if it was due to close before the magazine's publication date. An advantage of touring exhibitions is that a review can be linked with a showing at any venue.

Art market

The 'market' is a term used to describe the physical and social environment in which art is bought and sold. Similarly to any other commercial business, art is the 'commodity' and prices are determined by demand, although this can be manipulated by publicity and promotion. There is a complex relationship between those involved in buying and selling art, and auction houses, dealers and collectors all have a role to play.

The prices for which art works sell at auction determines price levels elsewhere. Most auction buyers are dealers who sell what they buy to collectors: "when they choose to buy a work from an auction house, most collectors still prefer to use a dealer as their agent in the gritty business of bidding." For the collector, the commercial gallery is a more comfortable place to purchase because the buyer can rely on the dealer for guidance and service.

Clearly, however "... the art market does not merely sell commodities but actively helps define what counts as art and particularly what is 'significant' art." The more acclaim, the higher the price for the work. The gallery's promotion is vital to raise the artist's profile and give the work an 'official' stamp of approval. Such promotion includes seeking substantial media coverage, encouraging purchase of work by major museum collections and collaboration with high-profile public galleries.

Relative Values, Louisa Buck and Phillip Dodd, BBC, 1991

Artists who choose largely to make art for idealistic reasons – love of making and personal satisfaction – believing quality will ultimately be recognised, can find these hard concepts to accept. However unwelcome though the idea of art work as product, it is vital to realise the power the market-place wields over the value of an artist's work. The concept of the market-place does not apply only to well-known artists whose work sells through commercial galleries. Any artist who sets out to sell work has a 'market' for it. As prices charged are largely determined by what the market can stand, ie what the buyer is prepared to pay, understanding the market for their type of work is essential for artists, whether selling at local, national or international levels or to friends, colleagues or collectors.

Moreover, artists whose work is not saleable cannot exclude themselves from the concept. As soon as artists seek an audience, they are reaching out to a potential market, whether that be the gallery audience or the host for an artist in residence project.

The K Foundation, described in *The Guardian* as "cultural terrorists", attempted to subvert the £20,000 1993 Turner Art Prize for the "best body of work by a British artist" (given to Rachel Whiteread) by awarding their prize of £40,000 for the "worst body of work" to the same artist. The foundation's claim is that the art establishment uses such awards to fulfil a cultural agenda whose prime objective is the preservation of itself. "The point is simple: art as a speculative currency, and vice-versa. To put it more bluntly: Art equals Money and Money equals Art."

Motivations & agendas

A combination of personal interests, aims and ambitions, working conditions and constraints contribute to the decisions and actions taken in relation to art and artists. These motivating factors are referred to as an 'agenda'. An artist's agenda may be to make art, safeguard their integrity and develop a reputation. A gallery director's may be to create exhibitions, run their gallery well and be seen to be prominent in setting trends. A critic's agenda may be set by the demands of a publication, their own interests in particular art issues and a desire to influence opinion.

It is important therefore for artists to be aware of factors which might govern the actions and decisions of an individual, for in any situation or working relationship, each person is negotiating a position based on their own agenda.

Affinities & allegiances

Within the art world, where a multiplicity of galleries, critics, artists, styles of work and issues of importance co-exist, those with similar concerns or common ground tend to strengthen their position by forming allegiances, establishing ways of supporting each other and of working together to mutual benefit.

Galleries with similar visual arts interests may exhibit a particular group of artists whom they see as a 'movement', and allegiances develop between these galleries and press and media where concerns and interests coincide, thus contributing to the development of that 'movement'. Whilst a number of galleries and critics may endorse a particular type of work or set of issues, others may dismiss these in favour of supporting a different group of artists and issues. Those involved in the process seek links with others with mutual concerns, creating networks locally, nationally and internationally, thus further developing a movement's profile. Artists also network with other artists, galleries and critics who share their concerns, exchange ideas and initiate exhibitions. Whilst a particular movement may dominate at one time, others develop concurrently and inevitably, as perceptions change, such patterns and allegiances also change. For example, an artform, gallery or approach which may begin as a challenge to the 'status quo' may end up as part of the establishment. A 'burning issue' may in time become a lost cause. Peripheral and difficult issues of one period of time may become main areas of concern and debate in the next.

Quality, money & power

Notions of quality, excellence, innovation and success are frequently used as justification for decisions, actions and support. However, these are questionable: different art world factions hold divergent views, these being coloured by personal preference, motivations and vested interests. The idea of mutual support between those with common interests is a sensible and often productive way for individuals to attain goals. Gallery directors and editors of art magazines describe theirs as a mutually supportive relationship, as a gallery whose exhibitions have been reviewed may support a publication through buying advertising and a magazine may want to allocate space for an exhibition review from a gallery which has regularly advertised.

There is, however, a fine line between mutual support and manipulation and control. For example, it is not unknown for a dealer to take out substantial advertising and then put pressure on a magazine to carry favourable reviews of shows by artists in whose work they deal.

More complex is the role of public subsidy in visual arts development. The vast majority of public funds go to national museums and major galleries and in turn, these institutions come to represent 'official' art history, established artists and accepted historical and contemporary trends. Recent Government policies have encouraged links between private and public sectors and on an individual basis, such collaborations make sense. A commercial gallery recognises the value of a collaboration which enables one of their artists to hold a major exhibition in a subsidised gallery which gets good media coverage. A subsidised gallery with limited resources might benefit through partnership with a private one in terms of producing publicity and promotional material or by receiving donations from commercial galleries and corporate sponsors. Inevitably, those with high profiles, influential positions and money to spend have the greatest potential for influencing others.

See also *Developing the Visual Arts*, ed. Eric Moody, City University London, 1994

Hierarchies & careers

The art world is composed of hierarchies which encompass galleries, magazines and artists. The multiplicity of values, criteria and opinions involved, however, means it is an impossible structure to 'chart'. Hierarchical positions are not necessarily based on quality, professionalism or profile and neither does showing at a 'good' gallery automatically lead to success.

A gallery's position on the hierarchy is, in fact, affected by their resources, publicity, track records of artists who show there, whether and where their exhibitions are reviewed, topicality of images or content of work, and equally importantly, the respect the gallery and its staff commands in the art world and the nature and status of the audience it attracts.

A library exhibition space intended as a resource for the community and showing work by local artists is necessarily lower on the hierarchy than a gallery appealing to an art audience and showing work by artists with national or international reputations. A review of an exhibition in a local paper holds a lower place on the hierarchy than one in a national newspaper or art magazine, and so on. Whilst, for example, the Royal Academy has consistently held a top place on the hierarchy, others may hold their positions briefly and are subject to fluctuations in fashion, viewpoint, popularity and money. Even more complex is the fact there are several hierarchies. For example a hierarchy of galleries showing issue-based work functions alongside another showing work of a more traditional nature and each of these has its supporters.

There are recognised ways of 'climbing ladders'. Artists who begin an exhibiting career by showing in a gallery low down on a hierarchical scale, may subsequently be picked up by a gallery higher up because it respects the first gallery's judgement. A gallery might build a reputation by 'discovering' new artists and promoting them to the art world. Well-organised and progressive galleries will use knowledge of such systems to their advantage and build contacts accordingly.

These hierarchical patterns also provide important career structures for those who run galleries and for critics and writers. Working relationships between galleries make it easier for staff to move on and up. In some cases, when staff move, they take their interests and artists with them and strengthen links between two galleries. A freelance critic with a close relationship with a gallery's work may gain a reputation for being an authority on the particular type of work they show and subsequently write about it for a specialist art magazine.

Changes & developments

The nature and make-up of the art world undergo continuous change and so do individual galleries. For example, Interim Art began on a modest scale in the East London home of its Director Maureen Paley. As her reputation developed, she gained financial backing to take premises in the West End. Later, she moved back to East London intending to combine her initial wish to show adventurous work by young artists with a more commercial approach. Central Space, originally set up by a studio group to show their own work, took so much time to run that one artist became a full-time director. Funding this post led to reassessment of policy and a decision to show artists other than those in the studios.

A change of staff can lead to new directions in programming. Although London-based Camerawork was first set up to meet local needs and interests and largely showed documentary photography on East End themes, when Sharon Kivland took over, her interests meant the programme changed dramatically to include experimental photography and installation. Subsequent directors built on this, and the current programme incorporates interests of the indigenous population as well as those of local professional artists.

Politics & economics

Political and economic climates have an enormous bearing on the state of the art world. During 15 years of Conservative Government and widespread adoption of their philosophies which encourage short-term values and quick profit, spending accelerated, auction houses and commercial galleries benefited as sales and prices escalated. The art market grew and young artists were sought and aggressively promoted.

However, government cutbacks have affected arts and local authority funding. Subsidised galleries and exhibition spaces have been encouraged to switch from 'producer' (artist-led) programmes to a 'consumer' (audience-led) approach. If they wanted public funds, they had to be seen to assess and understand their audiences, encourage new visitors and show a real interest in educational activities which bridged the gap between maker and consumer.

Recession beginning in the late '80s caused commercial investment to drop, and at the same time severe cuts in public subsidy continued. Subsidised galleries which had come to rely more on business sponsorship and on income from commercial activities and sale of work found competition stiff and fundraising hard, with the result that many reduced their programmes. Commercial galleries reacted by reducing risks and cutting prices and costs. Some, including those who simply hired out space, have closed altogether.

19

Recession, though, has provided some valuable alternative spaces and opportunities for artists' initiatives. In London's Docklands large empty spaces, impossible to let, have been used for artists' temporary exhibitions. This resulted in some galleries using such events to make contact with new artists and others collaborating with artists to organise exhibitions. Collectors had direct access to artists and the media's desire to cover new ideas focused attention on exhibitions which, had they been in regular galleries, may otherwise never have been covered. These kind of projects have now become an accepted part of the exhibiting network and an acknowledged place to look for new and adventurous work.

Gender

Although traditional art history once led us to believe there were virtually no women artists in the past, more recently, research and critical writing, mainly by women, has sought to redress the balance. The art world has traditionally been dominated by men as artists, gallery directors, critics and collectors but the last decade has seen significant increases in numbers of women involved in running galleries. With increased emphasis on equal opportunities and introduction of evening and part-time study, many more women have been able to practice as artists and makers. Women now make up 65% of fine art students and graduates but it is still more difficult for them to show, develop careers and climb gallery hierarchies. A survey by Fanny Adams in 1993 showed that 73% of solo shows in London galleries went to men and informal studies show that thematic, survey and historical shows still under-represent women.

Funds have been raised during 1994/95 to set up a Museum of Women's Art in London. The aim is to establish galleries and resource centre which reflect development through the ages of work by women artists in the UK and elsewhere, and to raise awareness through exhibitions and other events of the importance of women's visual arts work.

Whilst galleries at the very top still favour men, those lower on hierarchies tend to show a roughly equal proportion of men and women. Subsidised galleries often have equal opportunities policies, but female artists are still under-represented.   Many galleries maintain that gender shouldn't affect selection procedures. Imbalance tends to be explained away by justifications of quality. Elizabeth Macgregor, Director of Birmingham's Ikon Gallery, feels that men may be more successful at gaining exhibitions because "a male artist will not accept rejection so easily; if he really wants to show, he'll come back again and again until we look at his work."

With few role models in influential positions in art education, some women artists may lack confidence or be easily undermined. A late start, or time out to raise families, adds to the obstacles. Women also often seem less concerned with personal ambition and traditional measurements of success. They are, however, often particularly good at collaborative working and have good communication skills. As such abilities are a pre-requisite for taking on many of the new opportunities for artists – public commissions, residencies and gallery education – women's work is becoming more visible and is thus gaining respect elsewhere in the art world.

Cultural diversity

See also 5 •
Independent
curators

With few exceptions, the work of black artists has not been accepted by or integrated into the largely white art world. The Arts Council (now the Arts Council of England) developed a policy towards cultural diversity in the early '80s which led to the development of schemes to train black art curators and to establish black art galleries. One of the outcomes of this strategy has been the development of the Institute of New International Visual Arts (INIVA) which "explores work of artists irrespective of their cultural origin and regards their work as an integral part of a wider cultural debate."

Although some galleries have developed reputations for showing work by non-white European artists, the majority still do not. Some justify this by arguing that ethnic origin doesn't enter a selection policy which is based solely on quality. Café Gallery's Director Ron Henocq realises the gallery hasn't shown many artists of colour, "but we did not hear from many, and there are few in open studio shows. The balance is now beginning to be redressed, which I hope means more artists of ethnic origins will apply for exhibitions."

In the early '80s, artist Lubaina Himid undertook research into how black artists were treated by galleries and "discovered that black art was not a priority. They didn't know any black artists, they never went to exhibitions that black artists took part in. I just kept thinking to myself, well, blimey, I could do this. I know a lot of black artists, and I know people who don't 'know people', who are not taught by such-and-such an artist and can therefore get an introduction, who have a great deal of talent, a great deal to say, but don't have the 'ins'". In setting up the Elbow Room Gallery in 1986, her aim was to "get as many people as possible in there to see the work. What I'm really interested in is the thinking about it, the making it, the showing it, the talking about it, and the documenting it."

Bat Series 2, **cibachrome 1991 by** Tracey Holland, **from 'Touching the Light', City Museum & Art Gallery, Stoke on Trent September 1994, curated by Staffordshire University Women's Photography Project from work submitted for their photographic resource centre which is a long-term project aiming to recognise,.celebrate and research work of contemporary women photographers and writers on photography.**

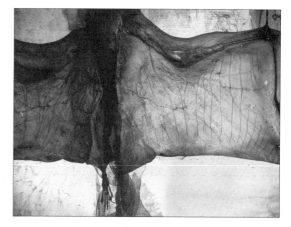

This exhibition formed part of 'Signals: Festival of Women Photographers' held September and October 1994 which co-ordinated and publicised over 300 exhibitions and events throughout the British Isles, and which aimed to redress the persistent imbalance in the representation of women's work within the profession as demonstrated for example, when the 1989 Royal Academy exhibition 'The Art of Photography' celebrating 150 years of photography included only five women out of 95 exhibitors.

State of the Art,
Sandy Nairne,
Channel 4, 1987

Indira Nandia at the Commonwealth Institute Gallery believes there are three types of black artists seeking to show: "the well-established like Sonia Boyce and Eddie Chambers who aim to be true to their origins whilst having a dialogue with the establishment; those who feel intimidated by the white gallery world, believing their ideas are not acceptable; and others who resist contact, refusing to be used as token gestures or to take the risk of their work being manipulated."

Age

Also discriminated against are older artists, many of whom see an active preference for youth in the art world, demonstrated by the competitions, prizes, awards and open shows which have age restrictions. But whilst some galleries sign up artists straight from college through degree shows and student competitions, others believe that maturity is an asset and watch artists' work develop over a period of years before making a commitment to show them. Younger artists are said by some galleries to need more support, and are less likely to understand the exhibiting process and sometimes lack confidence and professionalism. Young artists have also complained about not being taken seriously, that they feel overwhelmed by the range of opportunities or intimidated by repeated rejection.

Shifting centres

Although London is still felt by many to be the centre of the British art world as it contains the greatest concentration of artists, galleries and critics, Arts Council (now the Arts Council of England) policies from the early '80s attempted to redress the balance by increasing funding to the regions and giving regional arts boards more autonomy.

Installation by Lothar Baumgarten **at Transmission Gallery April 1994. Photo:** Simon Starling

Curated and administered by a committee of artists with support from members, the gallery aims to provide "a self-determined platform for promotion of the work of local artists and their national and international contemporaries. It has a particular interest in working with artists with new and unusual ideas who might otherwise not get the opportunity to exhibit."

Developments such as the establishment of the Tate of the North and the Tate at St Ives have helped to shift the focus away from London, as have policies to place art in public places. For example, percent for art policies – the principle of spending a percentage of the budget for new public buildings and urban regeneration on purchase or commission of art or craft – has been adopted by over 50 local authorities in England, Scotland and Wales.

Art publications now feature listings and reviews from around Britain and the Saturday *Guardian* has specialist arts guides for each circulation area. To counteract shortage of regular gallery spaces, artists in the regions have taken to initiating open studio days, visual arts festivals as well as other events which attract non-gallery audiences. Artist-run galleries including Edinburgh's Collective Gallery, Glasgow's Transmission and Manchester's Castlefield Gallery have gone from strength to strength. Some show established artists along with showcasing those in the area. Notably, inclusion in Transmission's exhibition programme has helped some artists to establish a reputation.

However, the call of London is strong and there is still a tendency for established artists to look there for major opportunities.

See also 2 •
Galleries &
exhibition spaces

Even high-profile regional galleries find it difficult to attract reviewers from predominantly London-based publications. Although many artists recognise the benefits of a show in a well-resourced gallery outside London where there is scope for large-scale and ambitious exhibitions or installations, they are nevertheless aware that their work may not actually be seen by those they want to influence.

2 • Galleries & exhibition spaces

In seeking to define the two thousand or so galleries in the UK, it is possible to describe them broadly as those which operate commercially and are running a business selling art works, and those which are subsidised in some way because of the benefits they provide to the public. But in attempting to analyse both types, it is clear boundaries are blurred; commercial galleries may receive subsidy for a specific project and subsidised galleries rely more and more on income from sales as well as grants and commercial sponsorship.

In terms of a working relationship, there is a good deal of cross-fertilisation between commercial and subsidised sectors. For example, notable commercial gallery directors are sometimes guest curators for exhibitions in subsidised spaces, and artists contracted to commercial galleries may also be shown in public spaces.

It is also possible to make a distinction between 'galleries' – spaces that are established to show artworks and have a member of staff with a definite role to plan and develop a programme in a cultural context – and 'exhibition spaces', whose role is essentially to receive shows made available by artists or other organisations. But again the boundaries are blurred.

Ultimately, it is not whether a gallery is 'commercial' or 'subsidised' which will make an artist want to stage an exhibition there. Choice is more likely to be focused on whether the gallery's concerns are in tune with the artist's. By describing the characteristics of different broad types of galleries here and by giving some 'sketches' of particular ones, the intention is to help artists to identify appropriate places to show.

Commercial galleries

The aim of a commercial gallery is to sell art or craft work, not only to survive, but also to return a profit to the owner, partners, shareholders or financial backers. Such principles affect not only what they show

External view of the Orbost Gallery, Dunvegan, Isle of Skye.

The gallery, which predominantly shows work related to the Western Highlands and Islands, is open from April to October. Prospective exhibitors are invited to send photographs of their work in the first instance to see whether it fits in with the gallery's 'image'.

and how they select artists but also what commission they charge, who is invited to previews and the 'image' the gallery presents to the press and media.

Some commercial galleries exhibit and sell only contemporary art, whilst others deal in 19th and 20th century art and also sell contemporary work. They may only show work by artists with whom they have regular contracts, or set out to exhibit many artists. Some make their reputations by showing international artists or particular styles of work, others may concentrate on 'younger' artists. Many show a combination of well-established and lesser-known artists.

Some have tiny spaces and others take over huge warehouses. Galleries, like the Orbost Gallery on the Isle of Skye, exist in isolated rural areas. Others form part of a 'cultural' area in a large city; London's Cork Street with its proliferation of galleries is an example. A gallery in an exclusive area inevitably has huge overheads and art work will be priced accordingly. Although another in a small town is likely to have far lower running costs, it may not have enough clients prepared to buy higher-priced work and subsequently will have to sell more work at lower prices for the gallery to be viable.

Private galleries

Although this term is used to describe commercial galleries, it also covers those which are not strictly 'commercial' because they operate with the benefit of some external financial input. Such galleries may be supported by the director's family, by a private income or perhaps be linked with an architecture or design practice. An example is Swansea's Mumbles Gallery which is run by architect Ian Campbell and maker Janet Campbell and shows work by local artists.

Andrew Lamont Gallery 65 Roman Road, London E2

A converted hairdresser's shop, this mainly shows small, affordable two-dimensional work which reflects the owner's interest in the locality. Selection is based on showing what he knows will sell and what he wants to show, whilst moving towards a greater proportion of the latter. The gallery aims to attract small collectors as well as locals making one-off purchases. Because he lacks resources to offer exclusive contracts to artists, his artists are able to exhibit elsewhere, and he sees this as mutually beneficial. Although he looks at slide submissions, most artists showing there come through personal contact. Artists contribute to promotion by inviting their own contacts to exhibitions.

Owners

Those who set up or run commercial galleries range from people with little initial knowledge of contemporary art who 'learn on the job', through to long-standing family concerns like London-based Gimpel Fils. Sometimes, a new gallery is formed when someone who has learned the business by working for another gallery leaves to set up their own, perhaps taking 'their' artists with them. Now closed, the Higherwater gallery in London was set up by a successful electrician who had worked in artists' houses and was motivated by interest in their work to use his business skills to start a gallery. Francis Graham-Dixon set up his gallery with a sound knowledge of contemporary art and a desire to show the work of artists he thought were under-represented. In some galleries, one partner takes responsibility for the visual decisions and the other provides the business skills, whereas in others, a sole director does everything from hanging shows to dealing with administration. Gimpel Fils employs nine full-time staff – mostly family members – and one part-time assistant.

Programmes

Exhibition programmes may combine different types of exhibition. A mixed exhibition – perhaps a 'Summer Exhibition' – is a commonly-used way for a commercial gallery to introduce clients to a 'sample' of work and an opportunity for them to try out new artists for possible inclusion in their portfolio. Group shows are more specific and tend to bring together a smaller number of artists with themes or links between work or approaches. Both methods are useful for broadening audiences and making new contacts as well for providing a platform for more artists' work to be shown. Group shows also help provide a

Art for Offices 15 Dock Street, London E1

This sells work predominantly to the corporate sector and shows painting, sculpture, prints, photography and crafts, split roughly 50:50 between abstract and figurative work, with prices ranging from a few hundred pounds to £20,000. Six exhibitions are shown a year in three galleries. In selecting artists, it takes into account the need for artists to be able to provide up to 20 similar pieces for a client. Peter Harris is one of several consultants who deal with how client needs for quality work can be balanced against budget.

It is relatively rare for craftspeople and designer-artists to exhibit and sell exclusively through one gallery. For example, Jane Hamlyn, who makes a living from her work, regularly shows and sells her ceramic ware in London at the Crafts Council shop, Contemporary Ceramics and Contemporary Applied Arts and in Harrogate at Godfrey & Twatt, as well as through other galleries and exhibitions abroad.

context and endorsement, for example for a new style of work. Solo shows, being an opportunity for the artist to show a body of work, are obviously the most prestigious though, more so if it is a 'retrospective' which charts an artist's work over a period of time.

Most commercial galleries have an annual programme of around eight solo exhibitions by gallery artists, with a mixed summer or Christmas show including other artists. Craft galleries in particular often advertise that they have a "changing display of work for sale." Whilst some specialise in print, photography or particular craft media, many make their selection on images, opting for figurative works, landscapes or work with a direct link to the location. Chantry House Gallery in West Yorkshire "specialises in painting and prints by contemporary artists, with particular interest in scenes of Yorkshire Dales and Lake District in oils, watercolours, pastels and prints."

Many directors, however, are unwilling or unable to define their programmes in this way since a great deal of intuition is brought to bear on selection and development of programmes. An interview with Nicholas Logsdale, Director of the Lisson Gallery, throws some light on his criteria: "No matter how talented someone might be, or however attractive their work, if it is covering well-worn territory it's never really going to find a place in the history books or the museums. And that to my mind is one of the most important considerations of what one decides to show."

Modern Painters,
Summer 1993

Audiences

Although a commercial gallery may have a relatively small and specialist audience, to survive it has to be aware of this audience, understand the best way to keep it interested and be able to cultivate

Gimpel Fils 30 Davies Street, London, W1Y 1LG

Long-established family firm originating ten exhibitions a year, mainly painting and sculpture with the occasional installation. A 'stable' of 18 artists including Albert Irvin, Niki de Saint Phalle, Terry Atkinson and Charles Beauchamp are on exclusive contracts which ensure they are shown regularly and are well promoted. Although some show and sell through other galleries, arrangements are handled by Gimpel Fils.

The gallery's varied audience results in sales to occasional visitors as well as regular purchases by British, American and European collectors. The West End location means the audience also includes students, artists and shoppers.

It makes a considerable investment in publicity and promotion which begins well before exhibitions open and includes full-colour cards and catalogues, magazine advertising, entertaining clients and reviewers which can run to thousands of pounds.

Although it largely shows established artists, the gallery occasionally takes on someone new, though rarely through application. An artist's development may be watched for years through group shows and close attention paid to how other artists and galleries talk about the work. Decision-making is lengthy and the gallery must weigh up what is involved in promoting a lesser-known artist against the fact that their work can't be sold at high prices initially and early shows may make heavy losses. Gimpel Fils believes the process is good for artists and gallery. It sees no virtue in signing up from college shows, as artists need time to mature and the gallery needs to know the work has lasting depth.

a relationship with the buyers. Francis Graham-Dixon knows it is important to spend a great deal of time with clients and visitors: "If first-time buyers walk in and the experience is good, they will come back." Anna Phipps of Austin/Desmond and Phipps which operates in London and Berkshire, comments: "In London we have passing trade prepared to pay a lot of money. Some shows outside London do well – particularly those of local artists whose friends and relatives buy – but here in London we tend to stick to what we know appeals to clients."

Galleries and artists

Exclusive arrangements – when an artist agrees that a particular gallery will be their sole agent – should be designed to benefit artist

Mono-print using inked up wooden blocks, stencils and collage by Steve Povall **shown at Printworks, Colchester in May 1994. His first solo show, 18 pieces were sold from the 31 mono-prints and two editioned prints exhibited.** Printworks specialises in the work of contemporary printmakers, often showing local artists because "there are so many good ones in East Anglia", and overheads are lower than when artists from farther afield are shown. Eight or nine one- and two-person shows are held annually, with work by about 50 artists kept in stock. The gallery promotes original prints as they offer the public a chance to buy a work of art at an affordable price, and tends towards the figurative. It also has considerable interest in artists' books and works on paper in general.

and gallery. A gallery's profile may develop concurrently with an artist's career. Although some artists establish a relationship with a gallery early in their career and stay with it, others begin with a small gallery and are later taken on by a more prestigious one. Some artists have no regular agreement with a gallery but sell work through a number who take work on a sale or return basis.

Angela Flowers Gallery, which operates from large spaces in London's East End – Flowers East and Flowers East at London Fields – represents between 25 and 30 contemporary artists. The relationship between gallery and artist is long-term and developing, with the gallery seeking to promote the artist in this country and abroad. In addition to solo shows by gallery artists, it also curates occasional mixed exhibitions around a theme, inviting artists associated with other galleries and non-aligned artists to take part. At Interim Art, Director Maureen Paley sees the relationship between herself and the artists she shows as a partnership, with both working towards a mutual gain and an equal interest in developing effective ways to promote work and generate sales.

Selection

Some commercial galleries clearly don't want to receive unsolicited applications. For example, London-based Thumb Gallery which specialises in paintings, drawings and limited edition prints, states their monthly exhibition programme "is by invitation only." Francis Graham-Dixon knew most of his artists before he opened the gallery,

Rib in leather and mixed media,
15" x ☜' x 7" by Mandy Havers.
Photo: Alastair Ogilvy

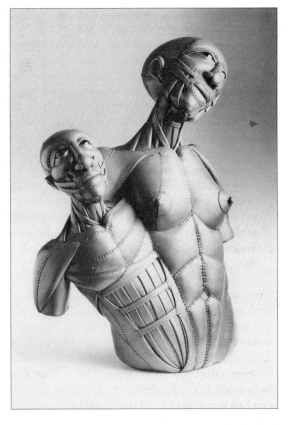

"**Although the days of the curator/dealer are now more or less over, there will continue to be a strong indication of the dealer's own taste and understanding in the way they group and publicise their artists. In my own experience, this has sometimes been at odds with the way I would wish my work to be understood. I have always found my dealer keen to discuss this and open to suggestions about positioning of works within a show. If an artist is eager to show and sell work regularly, compromises will sometimes have to be made.**"

having admired their work for some time. He does, however, take on new artists from time to time.

Commercial galleries often say they welcome applications although inevitably most get far more than they can handle and the majority of artists are found by other means. Most applications are looked at as they come in. Others save them up to be assessed once or twice a year which means that artists may have to allow for slides to be inaccessible for several months. Elly Robinson, Director of Printworks in Colchester, regularly looks at new work for her programme which often includes local printmakers who contact her and can bring in portfolios.

Advantages & disadvantages
Sculptor Mandy Havers has been with Nicholas Treadwell Gallery for 15 years and is aware of the danger of becoming 'labelled' which makes moving on difficult. Artists have also had problems when

significant changes occur in their work because if their early work has sold, a gallery may only be interested to keep them on if later work is of the same style. Although some galleries are able to accommodate such changes, there are examples of artists being given the ultimatum: "Continue making similar work or we end the relationship."

Regular shows don't necessarily mean a reasonable income and many gallery artists still don't earn a living from sales. Coventry painter Alison Lambert has an annual solo show with her London gallery Long and Ryle and must devote long hours over a concentrated period to meet exhibition deadlines. Although her relationship with the gallery brings sales, prestige and a regular showcase, she still has to supplement her income through her design business.

Selling the Contemporary Visual Arts, Gerri Morris, Arts Council, 1992

In spite of having a commercial label, a gallery may not actually be very good at selling. Gerri Morris' Arts Council research shows that many such galleries are not 'market orientated', and tend to rely on "artists, free listings and editorial to reach new audiences." Artists may, in fact, sell more work through self-organised opportunities such as an open studio event than they do through being contracted to commercial galleries. Conversely, however, involvement can lead to a wealth of opportunities. For Simon Edmondson, formerly with Nicola Jacobs and now with Benjamin Rhodes, advantages include the gallery bringing potential clients to his studio and chances to show work in international art fairs and exhibitions in Berlin, Zurich, Japan and USA. As a result of the gallery's ability to engage with the critics, well-known writers are commissioned to write his catalogue essays and his work has also been featured in major art publications.

See also **3 • Temporary presentations**

Subsidised galleries

Subsidised or publicly funded galleries are those which draw financial support from central or local government, arts councils, regional arts boards, educational institutions or from charitable sources. They are funded because what they do is perceived as providing a 'social benefit' – they have an educational role, they provide good PR for a borough council, they raise the profile of certain groups of artists, etc. Subsidised galleries may have several different roles. Some galleries will integrate these roles into a coherent policy, others give no thought to how they fit together. Galleries subsidised to run a contemporary exhibition programme include municipal art galleries where programmes of contemporary art are shown alongside permanent collections, specialist art, craft or photography galleries, arts centres where exhibitions may be shown in coffee bars or designated

Guildhall Gallery

Run by Winchester Museums Service, and largely financed by the local council, the Guildhall Gallery shows a programme of painting, sculpture, photography and crafts predominantly from local artists including three shows annually from Winchester Arts Club and a sponsored exhibition such as the Laing Open Exhibition which is essential for the gallery's survival. The rest is a combination of solo shows by local individuals and artists' groups.

Although the programme must be of interest to local people, a wide range of work including abstract and figurative work to a 'professional standard' is shown, with the most popular exhibitions being from the arts club.

The gallery's audience of between 24,000 – 30,000 a year is drawn mainly from those living and working in Winchester. Being located on the first floor is not ideal. Arts club shows tend to attract new visitors who may become regulars, and research has shown that the local *Time Out* attracts young people in.

Christopher Bradley, Keeper of Exhibitions, receives approaches from many individuals and groups. Although he looks at slides, he prefers to see original work and if it can't be brought in, he visits local artist's studios. Selection is made annually a year in advance, but with one slot kept free in case he later comes across interesting work worthy of showing.

galleries, galleries in libraries, universities and schools, galleries using former industrial buildings and heritage and rural crafts centre galleries.

Funding criteria

Local and regional public funding is necessarily linked with notions of social benefit and public access. For example, the artistic policy for Manchester City Art Galleries is based on a desire "to enlarge the audience for the visual arts in Manchester and beyond." However, local authority policies are subject to annual review and the fine detail of what will be funded, and to what amount, is often determined after much discussion and lobbying from arts organisations.

Regional arts boards in England have each determined their policies and priorities covering all artforms, and these are set out in five year plans. Northern Arts Board's policy to fund galleries whose programmes are concerned with increasing visual arts audiences is

Whitechapel Art Gallery

This is an independent trust funded by Arts Council of England, London Arts Board, local authority, trusts and charities with commercial sponsorship for specific exhibitions and projects.

Inevitably, sponsors tend to support events which interest them or are related to their product or services. For example, Becks supported Tim Head's retrospective because, as ex-Exhibitions Officer Paul Bonaventura said, "they liked his work so much" and his work "was also a useful promotional tool for them."

The gallery aims to provide a programme which responds to local cultural diversity as well as to the thousands of artists living and working in the area. These issues must be balanced with the gallery's international status and the need to mount exhibitions which attract worldwide interest and maintain funding levels.

The programme contains mainly solo shows of artists with international reputations, although the smaller of the three gallery spaces may be used to show the work of less established artists. Approximately every 14 months, the gallery organises the 'Whitechapel Open' exhibition, a mixed show of artists living and/or working in the locality which occasionally includes some craft work.

Outreach exhibitions of painting, sculpture, photography, installation, time-based work in local healthcare or educational settings are also organised.

The audience is local, national and international, although the extensive education and outreach programme is targeted at schools, community groups, artists and others living and working locally.

The gallery doesn't look at applications except for shows in local venues, these being handled by the education department. Suggestions for shows come from a range of sources. Gallery staff make an input and ideas often come from artists. Regular meetings discuss all possibilities, with Director Catherine Lampert having the final say. It may take several years for a particular artist to get shown though. For example, although Paul Bonaventura had been interested in Tim Head's work for many years, it was only in 1993 that he was given an exhibition. "It's really a question of context. You might take an interest in an artist's work and think it really deserves a show, but it just isn't the right time." By this time Tim Head was well-established.

Northern Arts Board: Exhibitions, Events and Commissions Scheme

"This supports the production, promotion and presentation of the visual arts and crafts. Scope includes one-off or programmes of exhibitions, events, public art commissions and curatorial initiatives." Criteria for funding are:

- artistic quality of the proposal including commitment to originality in form, content and presentation
- defined targeting of audience groups and/or participants, supported by appropriate marketing strategies
- contribution the project makes to critical debate surrounding the artform
- contribution made to programme development leading to Visual Arts Region 1996.

Open to applications from galleries, promoters, curators, local authorities and other organisations, the budget for 1994/95 was £144,000. It aims to support initiatives such as medium to large-scale exhibitions and touring; public art projects; temporary projects and performances and fixed-term appointments in curatorial or public art development.

Grants do not normally exceed 50% of the budget to a maximum of £25,000.

linked to the thinking behind 'Year of the Visual Arts' which the region is hosting in 1996. Criteria for funding includes the proviso that ideas and proposals must be trying to "change the way people perceive, relate to, or become involved in the visual arts."

Subsidised galleries, whether receiving regular funding or not, tend also to be involved to a lesser or greater degree with the time-consuming and unpredictable activity of raising additional funds from other sources including charitable trusts and business sponsors. To cut down on administration time and minimise rejections, many have developed finely-tuned fundraising strategies which enable them to ascertain whether the criteria of the potential funder or sponsor matches any of the activities the gallery wants to develop.

Gallery organisers

A gallery director or organiser in one of the larger subsidised galleries combines a thorough knowledge of the visual arts world with a portfolio of business skills which enable them to competently manage finances and staff, and write applications to gain new funding. They have to understand something about marketing and public relations too. Many of today's most experienced directors have learned these skills on the job and by working their way up the career ladder through

Commonwealth Institute Gallery

The Commonwealth Institute, housing the Bhownegree and Today galleries, has until recently been funded by the Foreign Commonwealth Office and can also receive funding from Commonwealth countries and private sponsors for particular exhibitions. Other galleries in the institute may receive funding from abroad if they mount an exhibition of an artist from that country or host a show originated there.

Policies are to show work by artists from Commonwealth countries including Britain and work linked to commonwealth issues.

Audience includes local school and adult education groups and visitors from abroad and the institute has a strong following from artists whose origins are not white British.

Applications come in throughout the year but are looked at annually by a panel of artists, academics and institute staff, all with affinities with the Commonwealth. Out of about 60 applications, in one day twelve shows are chosen for two galleries. There can, however, be conflicts. As the Institute promotes good relations within the Commonwealth, if an artist wants to show work about war, oppression or corruption within a member nation, Director Indira Nandia and committee have to make difficult decisions.

working with other galleries. It is only relatively recently that there have been specialist training courses in arts administration which deal with the practicalities of running galleries.

Many of those running contemporary galleries come from an art background with a fine art or an art history degree. The grounding in the field and the contact this gives them with artists is augmented by working with others experienced in managing a gallery space. Some, like Duncan Smith at Central Space, still continue to practice as artists as well as run a gallery. Alison Lloyd, now exhibition organiser at Middlesbrough Art Gallery, has a degree in arts management from City University and specialised during her course in gallery management. Chris Coppock, director of Cardiff's Ffotogallery used to be an editor of *Circa* magazine.

A local authority gallery may be run by a keeper who isn't a visual arts specialist. There is (at least) one example of a keeper in charge of a local authority gallery's contemporary programme having a degree in archaeology. Local authority library galleries may be run by people for whom administering the space is only a part of their job,

Central Space

London-based Central Space's exhibition programme is funded by the local authority and London Arts Board on the basis of an annual application – with no guarantee of success.

Although originally set up to show the work of artists with studios there, when they realised how much time the gallery would take to run properly, funds were sought to appoint a full-time director. "This meant we had to have a solid exhibition policy as no-one would fund just a group of artists wanting to show." As Director Duncan Smith was particularly interested in site-specific work and also had a commitment to providing a platform for local issues, these two strands became the basis for a fundraising strategy.

The gallery has seven shows a year of which six are solo and all are installations with local relevance. One is by an artist working at the studios, with five from other artists. A mixed show is mounted annually in collaboration with a local community group or school.

Selection procedures are lengthy and because they are tied with deadlines for funding applications, the outcome is unpredictable. Duncan Smith regularly sifts through submissions for those he finds interesting and suitable for the gallery. But with so few to select a year "even if I like an artist's work and would in theory show it, I can't give a definite 'yes' until I know I've got the funds for the year's programme."

other aspects being perhaps publicity and public relations. Whilst galleries in some universities are run by fine art department staff, others are run by contemporary art specialists like Claire Slattery who runs Leeds Metropolitan University's designated space. An unusual alternative to either approach is the Long Gallery at Newcastle University which has been programmed and run by students on the MA Fine Art course.

Selecting artists

Criteria and procedure for selection of work in subsidised galleries varies enormously. The biggest rarely select from unsolicited applications and most shows result from staff research and invitations to specific artists. In many, however, the programme evolves through a combination of recommendation and submission. Although some galleries are prepared to look at slides and work throughout the year, others have regular selection meetings and advertise these and any themes or particular styles of work they want to include.

New Scottish Art

This announcement from Centre for Contemporary Art in Edinburgh was published in *Artists Newsletter*, May 1994.

CCA is organising a three-month season for Autumn 1994 to feature interesting new art made by artists working in Scotland. To take place from 3 September – 26 November, it will comprise two or three separate exhibitions with the option of extra space being given over to time-based work, installations or video/film pieces.

Open to all professional artists working in any media in Scotland, the emphasis will be on art that is fresh and/or under-exposed.

Artists are invited to send up to ten slides, a statement about the work, what type of work you would be interested to present (no more than one page), biographical details and SAE or package for return of material.

See 9 • Approaching galleries

Galleries often comment on the number of applications they receive which are either irrelevant to the programme or badly put together. Many emphasise the importance of researching the appropriate venues to approach. As Indira Nandia at the Commonwealth Institute points out: "If someone doesn't read a form or fill it out properly they will probably be unprofessional and disorganised. I can often tell from letters if someone will be difficult to work with."

Advantages & disadvantages

Unlike commercial galleries, the role of subsidised venues is not to promote individual artists. The intention of their publicity and promotional material is generally to attract the public in rather than to satisfy the artist's desire to have a colour catalogue to show to other galleries afterwards. Quality of publicity material (design, copy writing and print) depends on the budget and staff skills available, and on the gallery's interest in marketing techniques.

In some galleries, artists receive a fee of up to £300 as an acknowledgement for presenting their work to the public. This concept is known as Exhibition Payment Right (EPR) and has some similarity to Public Lending Right for authors. However, despite attempts to gain widespread recognition of EPR and make it a condition of public funding to galleries, research indicates that less than 15% of galleries pay it and it is quietly falling into disuse.

Although some subsidised galleries (particularly those specialising in crafts) do set out to sell work, most are not geared to selling. Prices may be displayed, but on the whole, little attention is paid to nurturing potential buyers. The move towards creating installations means there may be no individual pieces of work to buy. Touring exhibitions also create problems for the would-be purchaser as exhibits will be needed for the whole tour which could last for many months. Exhibition previews are largely an opportunity for artists and the art world to swap gossip and enjoy the ambience. In some cases, the notion of 'marketing art' to new audiences is way down the priority list and is often felt to conflict with artistic policy.

However, subsidised galleries often reach wider audiences than commercial ones. Work may be seen by other galleries, collectors, and also gain media attention. For exhibitors, there are opportunities to take part in educational activities which not only generate income for them but also potentially create broader audiences for their work. Larger subsidised spaces may be able to provide more practical support than a private gallery. Some raise large sums from many sources including business sponsorship in cash or kind which they can use to finance more adventurous exhibitions particularly of installation, time-based work and performance art.

Because of the nature of their programmes, these galleries cannot develop on-going relationships with particular artists as can those in the commercial sector. In the case of the smaller-scale galleries, exhibiting artists may be required to assist in a range of ways including hanging their show, designing publicity and financing wine for the preview.

Artist-run spaces

Increasingly, artists wishing to have more control over exhibiting opportunities are setting up and running galleries themselves. Galleries have been established by artists in their own homes, by studio groups and also by groups who have found suitable buildings outside their workspaces. It goes without saying that artist-run galleries are supportive of artists and their work and because they know the problems and pitfalls from first-hand experience, are capable of providing practical and emotional help during the run up to the exhibition as well as when it's on. A comment by Café Gallery Director Ron Henocq summarises their attitude: "Artists find us friendly to work with. We want to help and support them, especially those who are younger or less experienced."

Such galleries are recognised as providing a kind of bridge for artists between showing in their studios and the established gallery sector. "Many artists we have shown early in their careers have gone on to make names for themselves." Adam Reynolds, who runs the Adam Gallery in London, feels that "artists are able to try out ideas in my space without feeling under pressure to succeed."

Café Gallery

A group of Bermondsey artists who began showing in a church hall later found a disused café space in Southwark Park which became the Café Gallery. Director Ron Henocq now has regular part-time secretarial assistance and a publicity person although temporary help comes mostly from artists: "We can't afford full-time salaries and flexible work can be useful to artists."

The annual budget of around £35,000 is covered by £30,000 in grants from Southwark Council and London Arts Board, with the rest earned through sales of work, catalogues, postcards, refreshments and a Friends scheme.

The audience is now wide-ranging. "When we started, we relied heavily on exhibitors' friends and acquaintances, but over the years we have developed a reputation amongst artists, other galleries, critics and writers from all over London and we also encourage community involvement through education projects."

The programme has local links as many of exhibitors are from the area or from Bermondsey Artists Group, and some have established reputations. It shows work which may be difficult to exhibit elsewhere, for example installations or work by unknown artists. At least one show a year is held in conjunction with local schools.

Ron Henocq and a panel of three artists select. Some exhibitions result from recommendations from other artists or from seeing work at open studios, group exhibitions and other artists' initiatives. "An artist I know and respect may suggest someone, I and one of the committee go to see the work. If it's interesting it's discussed at our next meeting although there may be further studio visits before we commit ourselves. Other exhibitions result from slide applications to the gallery followed by studio visits from the panel and me."

Many artist-run galleries begin with a group of artists who want to create more opportunities to show their own work – the Café Gallery in London, for example, was started by the Bermondsey Artists Group. These ventures generally begin with highly idealistic ideas about running a space as an alternative to established galleries. Initial energy and enthusiasm though can recede when the realities of running a gallery take their toll – long hours of unpaid work. Eventually many groups come to the conclusion that to survive they need to employ an administrator. Some, such as the Café Gallery, employ one of the original group members – Ron Henocq, now a paid

Adam Gallery

Adam Reynolds set up his gallery in the early '80s in his 18th century South London cottage using the shop front to show his and other artists' work. His relaxed attitude means he frequently modifies its operation to suit changing circumstances. Although in the past he ran it mainly single-handed, he has now established a voluntary management committee which includes five artists with an exhibitions sub-committee of four artists. Through these moves and the setting up of a Friends scheme, the intention is to secure the gallery's future in the longer term. Exhibitions tend to be solo and by less-established artists, chosen partly because of their work and whether it will suit the gallery's character, and partly on whether they sympathise with the gallery's more informal approach.

In terms of financing the gallery, although costs are kept to a minimum, income from sales makes a valuable contribution to overheads.

There is a mailing list, but the gallery largely relies on exhibiting artists to attract visitors. Regular visitors tend to have a connection with Reynolds, but locals do drop in.

director. In other cases such as Castlefield Gallery, Manchester an exhibition organiser is employed with the artists acting as a selection committee.

Pressures to raise funds to finance the shows can mean moving away from the original intentions – more shows by established artists or addressing contemporary artworld trends – in other words becoming part of the established gallery sector.

Cubitt Studios found a novel way to overcome this by inviting proposals from curators (who could be artists) who would select, organise and raise funds for their exhibition. Shows were to include both artists from the studios as well as others. A wide ranging programme resulted with the Cubitt Street Studios simply providing the space and selecting the proposals.

Artist-run galleries have come to realise how difficult it can be to deal with artists, as few have resources to promote individual artists or to nurture relationships over a period of time. As they tend to run on small budgets and rely on assistance from exhibitors, they expect artists to appreciate and accept the limitations. Audiences may come largely from exhibitors' contacts, so an artist may have to devote a good deal of time and effort to ensure their exhibition is looked at, listed or reviewed. Though galleries like Café and Castlefield, which

Castlefield Gallery

Run by paid staff and managed by a committee of artists, the gallery was set up by Manchester Artists Studio Association to "help people in the area enjoy art" and provide a gallery of national standing in the North West. Initially it relied heavily on artists' voluntary input but this became difficult when it conflicted with studio time.

Having developed a national reputation, the gallery attracts an audience from the region and elsewhere. The programme aims to show lesser-known artists alongside others with national and international reputations, trying to keep a balance between local artists' expectations and developing a challenging programme. Former Director Celia Cross believes this approach is good for gallery, artists and visitors.

The selection committee composed of artists receives many applications annually and looks at them once a month. Although exhibitions are selected from submissions, they may also arise from artists' ideas and from invitations to more-established artists. The gallery also runs an education programme and houses Slidex, an index of artists working in all disciplines, in conjunction with Liverpool Design Initiative.

Cubitt Studios

Set up in London by a group of artists who integrated gallery space into the studios, it solved the problems of financing the space by inviting freelance curators to select and organise shows and raise their own funds. Thus, income is a combination of a contribution from artists' studio rents with curators raising the rest.

They expect to mount a highly varied and unpredictable programme, since once a curator's proposal is accepted, studio artists have no control. It is expected, however, that the programme will include some studio artists, be a mixture of little-known and established artists and that all exhibitions will be thematic or mixed.

1000 visitors came to their first private view partly because, as artist Derek Harris says, "It is in the curators' interest to promote their own shows well."

now attract funding, are able to provide effective publicity, promotion and support.

Although few spaces have resources to promote individual artists or create a 'stable' of artists, Adam Gallery for example occasionally mounts mixed shows of previous exhibitors and Café Gallery's annual open show includes some regular exhibitors and others who've shown during that year.

Spaces in other contexts

Largely in response to artists' needs to have different types of environment to show their work to a wider audience, the scope and number of exhibition spaces has grown. Contemporary visual arts exhibitions can be found in cafés and bars, shopping malls and churches, nightclubs and theatre foyers and in heritage and sports centres.

Some of these spaces may look like galleries and be technically as well resourced, if not better. Others will be corridors or stairwells and may be used irregularly or once only. Some will be used for other functions as well – meetings, conferences or other community uses. Many do not have staff dedicated to programming exhibitions into the space. They may have permanent staff and regular shows – eg a library gallery – but the impetus for an exhibition will come from outside, probably from the artist.

Organisers

Whilst some who manage exhibitions in these spaces may know little or nothing about contemporary art and have limited practical knowledge of handling exhibitions or organising publicity, others are experienced and well-informed. Paul Hedge of Hayles Café Gallery trained as an artist and set up a gallery linked with a commercial venture to give him financial freedom to show work he supported.

He also works in the café and such a dual role is often the case for exhibition space organisers. Coventry University Gallery is run by the faculty administrator and Samantha Stevens, Manager at Leicester's Haymarket Theatre, says that programming the exhibition space represents less than a quarter of her workload.

Financing

Many exhibition spaces are financed by the host, that is local council, café or university as an integral part their main activity, with artists covering part or all exhibition costs. Freud's Café, for example,

Detail from Dan Geesin's **multi-media installation** *The Master Plan.* Photo: Julia Guest

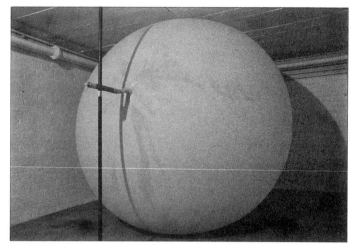

Sited in former GPO store rooms in Uckfield, East Sussex, the piece involved lowering the ceiling height by two feet using reclaimed waste and suspending it on electrical wires. One room held a weather balloon, inflated until it touched the walls, floor and ceiling with a gentle hissing sound filling the room as the air in the balloon escaped.

provides only space and some refreshments, although Coventry University pays all exhibition expenses and installs the show, with artists responsible only for framing and transporting the work. Many promote exhibitions through general publicity. The Museum of London produces a six-monthly events leaflet incorporating gallery exhibitions and Haymarket Theatre puts exhibition details in theatre leaflets, with artists handling any other publicity they want themselves.

Audiences

Although audiences tend to be the people who already go there plus the artists' guests, some set out to build a wider audience. Paul Hedge seeks to attract an art audience for café and gallery, and as a result, most shows have been reviewed. Like other educational venues, Coventry University's audience is composed largely of staff and students although locally distributed publicity aims to broaden the audience. Visitor numbers can be considerable: the Haymarket Theatre has 400 visitors a night, Museum of London between 22,000 and 26,000 a month, libraries up to 40,000 a week. However a minority will be interested in art and seriously look at shows. Sales may be good if the work is right for the audience and efforts are made to engage visitors' attention.

Programming

Public library spaces generally show work by local artists and work with local relevance. In such cases, the exhibition programme will be a mixture of amateur and professional, fine art and crafts, and solo and theme exhibitions. Bill Nuttall at Manchester Central Library

Timo Lehtonen's **studio at the Museum of London during a two-month residency at the Museum of London. Photo:** Museum of London

Focusing on **multicultural diversity and drawing inspiration from the historical perspective of the exhibition 'Peopling of London: 15,000 years of settlement from overseas', the residency included seminars and slide talks for groups and an exhibition in the studio of residency work.**

comments: "We consider all kinds of work. Exhibitions have included drawings, paintings, photographs and crafts, but we can't show anything too controversial." Haymarket Theatre wants to have a programme thematically related to drama productions and at Museum of London, shows must relate to museum activities and London itself.

Selection

Whilst the criteria at Freud's Café is to show work which appeals to the customers, Alan Humberstone's policy whilst he ran the gallery at Coventry University was to show mid-career professional artists from the Midlands or elsewhere who hadn't had a major solo show.

Library spaces tend to operate on a first-come-first-served basis, particularly where artists cover most costs. But the more the exhibition space offers financially, the more control they have over what is shown. Work which may in their view offend or be incomprehensible to library users may thus be turned down in favour of more accessible images.

Although Paul Hedge receives many requests for shows at Hayles, he "rarely selects from application – most people don't do their research properly. I receive applications from painters and printmakers, but as we only show installation in the gallery proper, when I suggest they might like to hang work on the café walls instead, they are offended!" He selects most shows through meeting artists who call in or through other artists' recommendations. In the case of Museum of London exhibitions, anyone who works there can suggest a theme, but artists also approach them with ideas. Coventry University Gallery annually invites submissions and receives over 400 applications which are considered once a year.

Advantages and disadvantages

Most of these spaces are not in a position to establish on-going relationships with artists or to promote the work of individuals. Although most have good relations with artists who exhibit, main complaints are that artists often apply without finding out enough about the space and its limitations. Those which require exhibitors to organise shows think artists' expectations are usually too high, and some also comment that artists aren't sufficiently organised. Similarly, artists may feel too much work is left to them or that organisers don't know enough about galleries, artists or art. Others are more positive and value chances to exhibit outside conventional galleries. But because many exhibition spaces need artists to take responsibility for finances and organisation, and publicity may not be exhibition-specific, exhibitors must generally put in considerable time and effort to make shows successful. However, opportunities to show are valuable for artists who have not shown before, especially when exhibition slots are allocated according to who asks first.

London-based artist Wendy Anderson points out the "need to be clear about why you show in this kind of space. It can be a good way to develop other opportunities, especially if the location is good and people find it easy to visit."

Early in my own career, I exhibited at short notice in a local architect's office. Staff were supportive, several bought pieces and one who collected contemporary art subsequently bought and commissioned pieces for his home. When he opened his own gallery, he offered me a show.

Such spaces can offer an engagement with a different audience to the gallery one. It gives many artists the only chance to have their work seen by the community in which they live and work. The space can provide a different kind of challenge to the work and an opportunity to 'try something out' that may not be possible in galleries wary of taking risks.

Smiths Gallery

Based in London's Covent Garden, Smiths hires out three galleries to individuals and groups. Shows, which are put on by artists themselves, include university degree exhibitions and the Contemporary Art Society's annual Artists' Market. Charges (1994) are £3,050 a week for Gallery 1 (1500 sq ft), £1500 for Gallery 2 (1200 sq ft) and £650 for Gallery 3 (550 sq ft), although daily rates are also available.

Situated in a busy shopping area, the gallery has built up a considerable reputation resulting in a wide audience and increased chances for artists to sell work.

Applications from artists are rarely turned down, and many who show there come back again and again because they have been successful. But Manager Jackie Remery comments, "These are mainly experienced artists. They know how to publicise and promote themselves."

Old Fire Station Arts Centre

This Oxford-based centre hires out a room for exhibitions which is also used for many different activities. Sometimes, and with the artist's agreement, these other activities may overlap with exhibitions. Terms are £100 a week or 25% commission (exclusive of VAT), whichever is the greater. As it also has a bar, restaurant and theatre, exhibitions may be seen by a wide-ranging but mainly arts-interested audience.

All this adds up to the need to view exhibition spaces as having a different role in an artist's career to the conventional gallery. Potentially these roles are parallel and an artist can move between them.

Hire galleries

Hire galleries range from rooms in private houses to large warehouse spaces. As some are purpose-built or have been well converted, they can be an effective method for little-known artists seeking to present their work in a better than average space. Although some take responsibility for selecting work from artists' applications, organising exhibitions and providing administrative backup, many others simply let space on commercial terms to artists who then organise, finance,

Crypt Gallery

A basement space at St George's Church, London, this is hired out at £25 a week plus 10% commission. Secretary Suzy Lake points out that audience depends largely on exhibitors' publicity. "Some don't realise this and expect far more than is reasonable – especially those from out of London who think a show in the capital will automatically bring sales and success.

"Anyone can apply to us for an exhibition, we look at all applications received." She, Father Michael Day and invited representatives from London art colleges look at slides, discuss work and select on suitability for the space.

promote and invigilate their exhibitions. Some take commission on sales as well as a hire fee. Usually, the audience changes for each show and attracting visitors to an exhibition is likely to depend largely on each artist's contacts and promotional skills.

Similarly varied are the credentials of those who manage them. Whilst Smiths' Jackie Remery previously ran a commercial gallery, Crypt Gallery's organiser learned the exhibition business on the job, having begun as secretary to the rector. However, as she has found the work interesting, if she moved job she'd like to stay in the exhibition business.

It is generally felt that more experienced artists stand a better chance of success, and that some exhibitors' expectations are unrealistic. Suzy Lake at Crypt Gallery comments that "many artists expect people to just walk in and buy work without any effort being made to encourage them. Some soon become despondent when there aren't many visitors. They become unapproachable and this puts people off."

Although hiring space gives artists freedom and control, where a gallery's policy isn't clear and there is little control over the selection, exhibitions are likely be varied in quality and experienced artists may find themselves showing alongside what they consider to be low-standard work. Artists who get the most from the situation tend to be "highly individual", because, says Jackie Remery at Smiths "they neither want to be restrained by a gallery nor pay commission." For artists who have good promotion and publicity skills and who have a clear idea of what they want to out of it, hiring a gallery may be a good option.

3 • Temporary presentations

Temporary presentations and installations encourage experimentation and provide artists with opportunities to address a particular theme or issue – social or physical – at a specific time. As a reaction to growing conservatism in the gallery world, there has been a steady increase during the last decade in the scope and number of artist- and agency-inspired temporarily-sited presentations, with many taking place, for example, in empty properties and urban wastelands.

Open studio events, often linked with arts festivals and mainly organised by groups of artists, are another kind of temporary presentation opportunity available to artists. These became popular in the '80s as artists became more confident of their ability to create and sustain their own presentation methods. Most are financed by the artists themselves and a mixture of public funds and private and business sponsorship, often given as materials or services rather than cash. London-based Robinson Road Studios' open days attracted small sums from the many local businesses used by artists, as well as occasional local authority funding, but artists still finance a major part of the event.

See also 'Sponsorship in kind', Fundraising: the artist's guide to planning and financing work , AN Publications

Audience response

Both Artangel Trust, and Birmingham-based Fine Rats International which generates live and public art events in sites of social or architectural interest, have been successful in attracting art world and other audiences. Media attention on Rachel Whiteread's House, a temporary piece in East London, resulted in a continuous stream of local and national visitors. Some days, hundreds of visitors descended with cameras and locals stopped to watch and comment. Responses on site were varied, some showed curiosity, others confusion or hostility, but many found it an "extraordinary" and "haunting" piece of work.

Fine Rats don't place too much emphasis on numbers or make-up of audiences. "They are important," says one of the artists Francis Gomilla, but "whilst we could hold an event without an

Artangel Trust

Artangel, which commissions temporary works in public places, aims to provide artists with challenging contexts in which to work. Projects have included slide projection, billboards, live art and temporary sculptural works. Originally set up with private, anonymous patronage to avoid political and commercial control, it now receives a combination of public and private funds and corporate sponsorship. Funds are often raised for individual projects and a commitment from Becks in 1994 has provided support for four years. Working relationships vary with each project. Many are suggested and initiated by artists. Negotiations can be long and involved and realisation of a project may take up to two years as ideas are developed and sites and funding sought. During this time the nature of a project may change dramatically.

audience, we feel an audience makes it work – gives it life. But we don't spend too much time monitoring. It's not a numbers game, it's the audience experience and contact with the work that is important." "We hoped," Simon Spain (Flotsam – Jetsam) observed, "to attract passers-by, but although a few local people popped in they usually left quickly – obviously feeling intimidated or that the work was incomprehensible."

Open studio events, because of the combined forces of the artists involved, frequently draw gallery directors, arts organisers and curators who can see a wide range of work with no pressure to respond. They also attract a curious local population who would not normally see contemporary art and love the opportunity to see behind the scenes. Inevitably though, media attention makes a big difference to whether the event achieves its aims. Because it is associated with the Whitechapel Open, the East End Open Studios has frequently attracted local and national coverage. An artist involved one year made contact with a writer on the *Evening Standard* who subsequently wrote a piece on her street; this in turn generated a local radio feature.

Successful collaborations

The most successful collaborations are when participants know each other well and have similar approaches and expectations. It is also helpful if everyone takes a relaxed and flexible attitude so that changes and difficulties can be accommodated, with people helping each other. Although not everyone involved in Simon Spain's project fulfilled their responsibilities, "it was very amicable. If someone couldn't do something, someone else just took it on."

Flotsam – Jetsam exhibition

Artists Simon Spain and friends persuaded the manager of a space in recession-hit Tobacco Dock, London to let them take it over temporarily. The result was a mixed exhibition of sculpture and installations related to the site by eight artists. It was financed by each artist putting in a small amount of money and other help in-kind rather than cash

Food Giant – Helen Smith

Helen Smith initiated an event involving local people and their response to their town in a Sunderland supermarket. From 5.30 am to 10.30 pm one Saturday she observed and photographed events over a two-mile circuit, including early morning workers, shoppers and football crowds, the six o'clock lull and the night life. She then spent two weeks in Food Giant creating panels of still images which combined with the moving images of the working supermarket. Whilst making the work, she engaged in conversation with staff and customers and found many fascinated by what she was doing and keen to relate historical and contemporary experiences of the town.

All costs including artist's fee were financed by Sunderland City Council Arts Unit, one of a network of 33 Local Arts Development Agencies (LADAs) created in Northern England through funding partnerships between Northern Arts Board and individual authorities. The arts officer was "very supportive: I could call her any time". The supermarket manager's interest in art as well as in a good publicity exercise helped. Location brought a guaranteed audience: being just past the checkouts meant she couldn't be missed. "Response was fantastic. People were so curious and I spent a great deal of time listening to personal experiences of Sunderland."

Advantages and disadvantages

Artist-led initiatives can provide a relatively quick way to show, gain experience and make fruitful relationships. Simon Spain now feels, "On the whole I wouldn't want to show in any other context. This way, you have control over the look of the show, publicity and how much you put in." Terry Smith, who also took part, observes: "Working with others in a space helps develop your ideas, it's interesting and challenging to listen to others' ideas about what you are making. I changed my piece several times as a result of the dialogue."

Speculation by David Friar **who is contributing to the Aerial programme during 1994.**

A newly formed artist-led organisation, Aerial is mounting a series of events leading to a programme in 1995 when 100 artists will be commissioned "to permeate the city of Edinburgh with visual art, transforming it into a fully-integrated arena for creative activities which will engage with the public in its own space." To get this initiative off the ground and raise the amount of public and private money needed has meant a considerable amount of personal 'sponsorship' from the organising artists. They anticipate, however, that in the future these costs will be covered by income raised for events.

Open studios have become a very important aspect of many artists' career development. One year, a Robinson Road artist sold £2,000 worth of work, whilst another in Beck Road was subsequently taken on by the Anne Berthoud Gallery. However results like these are rare.

Self-generated events can take up much time and money, sometimes causing a conflict of interest between making and organising. Helen Smith spent many months finding someone interested in her shopping centre project, with several possibilities falling through before the local arts development agency (LADA) took an interest. She says, "It was gruelling but you have to be persistent. I may not find the partner I need to allow a project to happen but that doesn't mean it's a bad idea – it's just that the climate is wrong. So I'll keep an idea on file to return to."

Agencies which take on organisational and financial matters leave the artist free to develop ideas and make the work. The nature

From the installation *Feng Shui*, **influenced by the ancient Chinese practice, sited at All Saints Church, Newcastle upon Tyne by Canadian artists** Paul Wong, Lani Maestro, Sharyn Yuen **and** Henry Tsang. **Curated by Elspeth Sage and commissioned by Locus +. Photo:** Simon Herbert © **Locus +/the artists**

As part of a lecture tour in Ireland organised by Locus +, a video screening of Paul Wong's *Chinaman's Peak: Walking the Mountain* **and a public lecture on Feng Shui formed part of a programme of events accompanying Belfast's Flax Art Studios open studios exhibition.**

of some projects however, will mean artist and agency sharing the organisation and even some of the funding negotiations. Staff who are skilled negotiators can smooth the way with funding and other bodies who have the power to decide whether a project happens.

The major advantage for an artist of initiating and organising their own show is keeping control. Control means hard work – and a lot of it – but it also means that, within your resources, you are more likely to get what you want. And for some artists, of course, that 'organisation' is seen as part of the production process. For them the office becomes the studio, the telephone becomes a creative medium. When artist Susanne Silver described an installation project she organised in Aberdeen to artists at a National Artists Association conference, she was asked how much time she spent on 'administration'. Some artists were shocked when she said that 90% of her time could be spent on 'admin'. But, as she pointed out, without that 'admin' the work would never happen.

Whether operating through an agency or managing their own projects, artists must be confident about communicating and establishing working relationships with others, especially those who are not directly involved in the art world. Getting a project off the ground is often a lengthy and complex process and it may flounder altogether unless the interest of all those involved is maintained.

4 • Open exhibitions

The term 'open exhibition' describes shows which have an open submission, that is, when artists are invited to put their work up for selection. It includes annual or biennial survey exhibitions which may be thematic or which aim to show a representative sample of contemporary visual art or craft work. They range from the internationally-known John Moores Liverpool Exhibition, open to painters nationally, to Christmas shows in private galleries, and are variously described as lotteries with unfavourable odds or important opportunities for less-established artists.

Whilst most include one or two works by each artist, there are exceptions such as 'East', the annual exhibition mounted by Norwich Gallery, at the Norfolk Institute of Art and Design in which selected artists may be offered space in the institute's studios to show a body of work or create an installation. The 1993 exhibition catalogue stated

Whitechapel Open

In 1992, the Whitechapel Open, which invited submissions from artists living and/or working within specified London postal code areas, included painting, sculpture, prints, photography and installation. The 1810 entrants were charged £5 each, with exemption for unemployed artists. 191 artists' work was hung and about £8,000 raised from fees. The exhibition usually attracts a commercial sponsor to contribute to the overall budget of over £50,000.

Selection took a week, with a panel of six including two staff members, artists and one other looking at work three times. At the first stage, interest from any panellist keeps a work in, but by the last stage four or five of the selectors must support a work to keep it in.

Frequently, sponsored prizes are awarded for the 'best' work in specific categories.

Dan Gardiner, *Switch*, **mixed media/canvas**

"Opens vary enormously in terms of the work which is shown; this is due to the regulations and concept of each show, the selectors and the artists who submit work. All these factors can include or exclude many of the facets of art making today. In 1989, I was included in the Whitworth Young Contemporaries which contained painting, sculpture, installation and video and in the John Moores 16 which showed exclusively painting. Although I was a prize winner in both, being in the latter had greater significance. Opportunities which arose included a five-day open studio during the showing at Walker Art Gallery, visiting lecturing at Liverpool Polytechnic and Wirral College and exposure through reviews in *The Guardian* **and in art publications. Since beginning a 2-year MA at the Royal College of Art, I have frequently exhibited in London, including in Cork Street."**

that "we wanted to create an exhibition with no rules, which respected artists and enabled them to show a substantial group of work." The show which has always been open to national submission will in the future be open to mainland European artists too.

Some opens are part-invited, an example being the Royal Academy Summer show which invites Royal Academicians to submit work. The Café Gallery's annual Christmas open guarantees to hang at least one work by each entrant, although size restrictions are imposed. Open exhibitions are largely financed by the organising gallery, with artists paying an entry fee and/or a hanging fee. Prizes, which vary in value from a few hundred pounds to several thousand, are often enabled through sponsorship. Entry fees vary enormously too: the Café Gallery charges £3 per entry, others may charge £15 or more.

Opens are advertised, mainly in the art press. *Artists Newsletter* has a regular monthly listing where you'll find most open exhibitions and competitions, national, regional and some international.

55

John Moores Liverpool Exhibition

Sponsored by the John Moores Family Trust, sponsorship, sales of catalogues and posters and 2,000 entrants paying handling fees of £10 cover less than half the cost of organising and mounting the show, with Walker Art Gallery financing the rest. Keeper Julian Treuherz comments, "This is the most expensive exhibition in our programme."

Works are delivered to four collection points and then transported to Liverpool and artists can also bring their work to Liverpool themselves. A selection panel of three or four people drawn from artists, gallery staff or others involved in the visual arts spends a week choosing. Two days are usually spent in looking at all the entries once; the rest of the time in reducing those identified as possibilities to a show of about 60 works. Two weeks are spent repackaging and returning rejected works to collection points.

First prize is a £20,000 purchase and there are ten cash awards of £1,000.

East

In 1993, Norwich Gallery looked at 8,000 slides by 800 artists. The exhibition catalogue stated that selectors – artists Konrad Fischer and David Tremlett – "responded to art that was 'good of its kind', making their selection from the slides, only requesting more information about scale or substances."

Advantages & disadvantages

Audiences for open exhibitions include those who normally go to the gallery along with each selected artist's guests and supporters. Open exhibitions tend to gain media attention, though often get bad reviews. An advantage for exhibitors is that they are used by galleries, arts organisers, agents and freelance curators to 'scout' for new artists and also by educationalists to find guest lecturers or visiting artists. Julian Treuherz, Keeper of Art Galleries, of Walker Art Gallery feels that being hung in a major open will be considered a gain for most artists and comments: "Having the John Moores on your CV is generally felt to be an advantage." Some opens produce good catalogues, for example 'East' and 'BT New Contemporaries', and these can be useful promotional tools for an artist long after the show has finished.

Eastbourne Biennial

Run by the Towner Art Gallery in Eastbourne this show is open to artists in the south east of England and is always based on a theme. The last open had the theme of 'Interiors' which artists were asked to interpret widely. The gallery feels the theme helps give the show some unity that allows quite a mixed audience to respond to a broad range of work. This often means the audience is less dismissive about experimental work. Selection is from actual work, rather than from slides, and about one third of the work submitted is shown. Last years selectors were Bill Feaver, the Observer art critic, artist Eileen Cooper, and Penny Johnson, curator of the Towner. They made a further selection and Mary Cozens-Walker and Rose Wylie were offered solo shows at the gallery. The prize of a solo show is interesting and unusual and is a regular feature of the open.

However, in most cases, the odds of being selected are low. Work chosen is likely to reflect the interests of that particular year's selectors. Although entry fees remain low in relation to exhibition costs, the added costs of framing, packing, transport and even insurance can mean a significant investment. Each individual artist must weigh up the relevance to their work against the costs and selection odds.

5 • Independent curators

Although independent curators may be former exhibition organisers or ex-directors of galleries, they can also be artists, critics, writers or academics. They may put together exhibitions regularly or occasionally, some using temporary spaces and others conventional established galleries.

For Cornwall-based artist and lecturer John France, 'Peninsular Journeys', a touring exhibition for university galleries, was his first experience of curatorship. Kay Roberts, on the other hand, has established a national and international reputation as a curator. Writer and editor Amanda Sebestyen puts together theme shows of work she admires, often combining a core exhibition of a few artists showing a body of work, with others contributing one or two works. Although she often uses galleries, one of Kay Roberts' collaborative projects was 'An English Summer', sited in historical buildings such as Palazzo Ruini, Reggio Emilia in Northern Italy. Amanda Sebestyen often seeks 'alternative' venues which she feels are sympathetic to her political and social themes.

Financing exhibitions

Independent curators, like others in the subsidised sector, must seek finance to carry out their projects from multiple sources. Some ask for a contribution to costs from artists, although most don't expect this. John France feels that if an exhibition is his idea, he should take financial responsibility. "Although Coventry University financed the catalogue and the showing at their venue, I made a loss and put it down to experience. It was just something I had to do."

Kay Roberts says it is essential to raise money to pay artists a fee over and above organisational costs. As her projects involve installation, "artists have to make work especially for the site which can involve a great deal of time and expense. Even though I pay a fee, I know it may all go on making the work." Her projects have attracted both public and private funds. Some have been collaborations, with a host venue sharing costs.

Untitled photograph by Samena Rama **whose work was featured in 'Disrupted Borders', curated by Sunil Gupta for the Institute of New International Visual Arts and shown at Arnolfini and The Photographers' Gallery in 1993. Photo: courtesy Panchayat for the artist's estate**

Sunil Gupta is an artist, photographer, curator and cultural activist who has been organising exhibitions since 1986.

Independent curators may also be able to access arts council or arts board funding aimed at generating research into exhibitions. For example, the Arts Council of England's Live Art Travel and Research scheme enabled independent curator Helen Cadwallader to visit North America to investigate a networking exhibition to contain work by UK and international artists and planned for 1996.

Finding artists

Artists in independently-curated exhibitions tend to be found through personal contact. In Kay Roberts' case, "I work with a small group of artists whose work I know well, although this may change over time. It is essential to work with artists to whose ideas I relate. It may be years after first seeing their work that I show them though." She explains that "curating a show is much more than just selecting work you like. It is the ideas linking the work which provides a framework. The curator's job is to make links through an in-depth knowledge of each artist's work."

John France also selected largely artists he already knew for his idea based around living and working in rural areas. London artist friends had been invited to stay and make work, and he also got to know and like local artists' work. From that starting-point, he looked for others whose work suited the theme. Amanda Sebestyen's knowledge of artists had grown through a period of writing for *City*

Limits. Some artists she has shown were those whose work she saw and admired then. For one exhibition organised in aid of CND, she asked the organisation to put her in touch with artist members who might be interested.

Advantages & disadvantages

A major advantage for artists of working with independent curators is flexibility combined with support. Cornelia Parker who has shown with Kay Roberts comments: "It was a good opportunity to explore more adventurous ideas. Kay gave practical support whilst giving me the space to manoeuvre." If the relationship works well, artists are more likely to be included in a curator's subsequent events. Curators also help by developing a context for new or difficult work, something which many artists would not be able to do for themselves. In terms of helping artists up art world hierarchical ladders, being shown by independent curators brings greater exposure. Two of the artists shown by Amanda Sebestyen, for example, have subsequently developed successful careers.

However, as it can be hard to raise funds for independently-curated exhibitions, artists may not be well-rewarded for their endeavours. Amanda Sebestyen, for example, is unhappy she has been unable to pay artists who have made work especially for her projects, knowing many have also put in unpaid time to help. She has also found it difficult to create media interest because "I tend to like work which is not currently in the public eye." Although she puts as much time as she can into promotion, she acknowledges it needs more.

As independent curators often take similar approaches to artists, that is they are adventurous, take risks and try things out, many sympathetic relationships have developed of mutual benefit to artist and curator which have resulted in exhibitions which would not have been shown in more conventional circumstances.

6 • Sales commission

For commercial galleries, commission from sales may be the only source of income other than the owner's or partners' investment. And whilst some may make substantial profits, others struggle to survive. The appearance of the director's lifestyle may be deceptive because whatever the reality, an aura of success must be displayed to maintain the confidence of buyers, funders and promoters. Even the best-known galleries suffer fluctuations in sales and are affected by the economic climate. Subsidised spaces are equally under pressure. Reductions in public spending result in cuts to gallery budgets and greater emphasis on earned income, sponsorship and commercial viability.

But as part of their aim to try to maintain an equal relationship with galleries, artists have to take into consideration all the implications of exhibiting and selling, including arrangements about the percentage of commission on sales.

For a detailed explanation of sales commission techniques, trade and retail prices and VAT implications, see *Selling*, Judith Staines, AN Publications

Sales commission can range from as little as 10% of the selling price to over 60% in top commercial galleries. Most fine art galleries ask artists for the selling price of a work and deduct a commission from it, but in craft and design galleries makers are generally quoted a commission rate (or mark up) of between 50 – 150% which is added to the figure the artists wants to receive for the work. In some cases, artists at the same gallery have different agreements about the percentage of the sale price which will be taken by the gallery. The confusing issue for the buyer can be finding an artist's work differently priced in different places and that can have adverse effects on sales. It can be better to price your work so that the 'retail price' (what the customer pays) is consistent even though this means you receive different prices from different galleries.

Ideally, the percentage taken should be linked to the degree of responsibility taken by a gallery. As a rough guide, if a gallery requires the artist to do all organisation and pay all costs, commission should be small, say under 10%. If these responsibilities are shared

See also *Introduction to Contracts* and *NAA Public Exhibition Contract*, AN Publications

it might rise to 15-20%. If the gallery bears most responsibilities and costs and the artist deals with framing and transport, it could be 30 – 40%. If, however, the gallery takes full financial and managerial responsibility and promotes the work well, they are likely to take 50 – 60%. Be on guard against a gallery which charges high commission and expects the artist to pay substantial exhibition costs such as those connected with publicity.

High commission rates often elicit protests from artists since this can be a large slice of the selling price. But as the selling of work may provide the only income for the gallery, the owner must see a return for his or her efforts. The important questions are: does the work sell, what income would be made from those sales and is promotion effective and appropriate to your career? The answers to these questions establishes whether the artist gets 'value for money' from a gallery. Simon Edmondson, who shows with Benjamin Rhodes Gallery, comments: "I don't know enough people who could afford to buy my work at even half the selling price. Without the gallery I couldn't make a living from my work."

Whilst most galleries behave fairly, artists do have to guard against the few unscrupulous ones. The figures above are only a guide, and each artist is responsible for checking out a gallery's offer well in advance of an exhibition and before making any agreements. When the negotiation is complete, the best way to seal it is through a contract or written agreement which clearly states the terms.

7 • Education & interpretation

Subsidised galleries have a considerable interest in running educational activities alongside exhibitions and events, seeing them as a way not only of broadening audiences generally, but also of engaging with schools and communities and influencing future attitudes to contemporary visual arts. An education programme may include artists' residencies in or outside the gallery, intensive workshops for children, teachers or other groups, demonstrations and lectures on particular artists or issues surrounding an exhibition.

Recognising that education starts with information, like many other gallery organisers, Anna Pepperall, visual arts manager at Gateshead Libraries and Arts, accompanies exhibitions with "an explanation of the show, detailed labelling and, if appropriate, an explanation of the artist's working methods and processes." The Libraries and Arts department, which manages gallery spaces, residencies and other events has done much work with people with learning difficulties and runs a programme specifically for older people. Participants get to know exhibiting artists and are encouraged to take part in artist-run workshops with the resulting work often exhibited. As well as Saturday workshops and demonstrations, she runs residencies in schools and other community settings which often generate exhibitions. "After a residency has ended, groups are encouraged to continue and some financial assistance is given so they can continue to work with artists."

Camden Arts Centre runs an ambitious programme of half-day schools workshops, classes for other groups and gallery-based residencies, as well as talks by artists and critics. This runs in parallel with the exhibition programme and relates directly to exhibitions. Education Officer Laurie Peake draws artists from a large pool and the programme is partially designed to help inexperienced artists gain skills. Artists are chosen to work alongside specific shows because of links with their own work. Residencies are similarly selected, although the residency format depends on each artist. In Steve Nelson's

Hand-hooked tufted rug 64" x 43" by Sara Worley. **Photo:** the artist

Workshops in rag-rug making, stump work, embroidery, textile painting and spinning aimed at young people aged 14 and over were held at Maidstone Library Gallery to accompany 'Boundaries', an exhibition of embroidery, weaving, recycled textiles, tapestry and rag and tufted rugs by the Strictly Textiles group of Angela Harrison, Hayley Smith, Lesley Millar, Lizzie Reakes, Sara Worley, Sarah Wiggs, Veronica Tonge and Deborah Walker, who invited Ann Taylor to exhibit with them.

residency, coinciding with a Pistolletto exhibition, he made his own work and spent two days a week working with special needs school groups. Jo Stockham, however, worked on an installation during her solo show, with visitors seeing it taking shape and able to come to the opening at the end. Saturday art classes are a regular feature, usually with one artist running them for a term or a year. These are seen as an important way of introducing young people to galleries and contemporary art.

Café Gallery has a modest but interesting education programme, with activities organised for schools and community centres with local and exhibiting artists involved. Two exhibitions annually show the resulting work by artists and participants and the gallery is therefore able to demonstrate to a wider audience how involvement with practising artists promotes creativity in others.

Value to artists

Overall, artists find working with gallery education programmes a rewarding activity. Simon Callery, who began working with the Whitechapel Art Gallery in 1988 and now works with other galleries' programmes recognises them as a chance to reassess his work and see it from new perspectives, and also as a way of looking in depth at issues surrounding his and other artists' work. It has also helped him develop confidence in working with people. A show at Anderson O'Day Gallery resulted from a Camden Arts Centre residency, although he's quick to point out this isn't a reason for taking on such work: "You have to want to do it for its own sake. Spin-offs are a bonus."

But in undertaking educational work, Laurie Peake explains that "artists are not teachers, they offer a very different set of skills and experience related to their practice." Simon Callery agrees: "You need to be able to get them to be quiet and concentrate and do things in an exciting way without temporarily stepping into the role of teacher and without losing your identity as an artist." Gallery educationalists are looking for artists who have ideas, who can structure a workshop, communicate with and enthuse an often young audience and who can generate and sustain participation. Anna Pepperall comments: "With increasing workload on arts staff, organisation is often left to the artists, although this is obviously negotiated and the costs of such work will in future be built into budgets, which is already the case with the time spent on preparatory work." She also looks for artists whose work has "reached a certain standard and direction", something especially important for long-term residencies.

8 • Self-assessment

The art world is a complex and constantly shifting set of networks and contacts, a situation which photographer Rhonda Wilson has described as a "fast-moving standing space with no easy chairs."

The criteria used by galleries in selecting artists may be difficult to define or understand; most find artists through a mixture of personal contact and recommendation. Although some artists feel this is unfair and favours particular types of artists, it is the case that criteria used to judge quality are subjective, and galleries must be able to make decisions in the less formal, personal and organic way that suits them.

Each artist, gallery or organisation has their own 'agenda' based on personal, professional and financial factors, and working relationships are based around assessing common interests and aspirations and defining mutual benefits. Artists need to recognise this and the most successful use personal research and contacts to find opportunities for their work.

To develop their careers, artists are likely to be involved in promoting and selling their work through different types of exhibitions, trying to get media coverage and reviews, seeking public recognition through, for example, undertaking commissions, fellowships, doing lectures or teaching whilst also using their transferable skills to run workshops or work in the community.

Artists who feel they have no contacts or inroad into the art world may see it as impenetrable and 'success' an impossible dream. But those who make the decision to take responsibility for the development of their careers, use the complexity and variety of opportunity to carve out something for themselves. The importance of good preparation can't be emphasised enough. Approaching galleries requires confidence, understanding, good communication skills and excellent presentation. The next two chapters explore ways to achieve these.

Strategy

There is much more to being an artist than making work. To show and develop a career involves a combination of knowledge, understanding, decision-making, actions and skills. Many devote minimum thought to approaching galleries, making applications almost arbitrarily. Although luck may bring a show straight away, more likely is rejection and a great deal of wasted time. A carefully worked out plan may seem time-consuming but saves time overall and will reap greater rewards. Such a strategy means no more than facing reality, self-assessment, research and working towards goals, all happening concurrently but in different combinations: a creative process.

Questions to ask yourself

Self-assessment is essential if you want to realise ambitions, and can help throughout your career: for example, when you've not shown recently, if all approaches have been rejected, when too many tangential opportunities have arisen and you've neglected your work or if your time is swamped by projects no longer in tune with your interests or situation. Answering the following questions will help you look at yourself, your work, where you are now and where you want to go and are the basis of a personal strategy for change.

What kind of work do I do?

You may be able to say whether you make small or large-scale work, paintings or installation, figurative or abstract, but can you define the content, subject matter or concerns? Are you more interested in traditional values or do you relate to the avant garde? Is your work object- or issue-based or conceptual?

In what context do I see my work?

Do you imagine your work in a commercial setting or public site? Is showing for its own sake important, or are you interested in communicating with a specific audience? Where and when have you seen the work of other artists you relate to? Can you identify a historical and contemporary context for your work? Do you see yourself showing locally, nationally or internationally? How do you see yourself in relation to art world trends?

Why do I want to exhibit?

Do you want feedback, to communicate with an audience, sell, develop new ideas, carry out work which needs a particular kind of space, further your career, develop a reputation or provide other specific opportunities?

How important is it for me to show?

Is making the work most important, and exhibiting a bonus, or is showing essential to work? Would you make art whether you exhibited or not, or do you only make work specifically to sell or show?

How much time can I devote to it?

Do you have time to research, make approaches, develop a dialogue with others and see through practical responsibilities? Do other responsibilities limit your time?

What are my long–term aims and ambitions?

Imagine where you'd like to be in five years time. Do you want to make a living from sales, gain national or international recognition, develop a fulfilling and enjoyable career or a combination of these? Do you identify with others who have achieved things you would like for yourself? Think about specific galleries, types of projects or job situations you are aiming for.

What do I have to offer?

This can include transferable art skills like welding and paper-making, or organisational skills such as typing, and personal attributes like patience, ability to communicate well, or an interest in environmental issues.

What are my weaknesses?

Do you lack confidence? Is your documentation below standard? Do you find it difficult to work with others or dislike the idea of promoting yourself? Are you unaware of local opportunities or what goes on in the art world?

The following are questions you might ask yourself each time you want to try for an exhibition or feel the need for a change of direction in your career.

What do I want from my next exhibition?

Are you seeking critical acclaim, an opportunity to reassess and gain feedback? Do you need a specific kind of space to try out a new idea. Do you want to show outside your area? Are you looking for a new audience or seeking commissions? Do you want a more prestigious gallery or to attract particular individuals to see your work?

Am I ready to exhibit?

Do you have a coherent body of work? Do you feel confident about your work and your ideas and able to articulate them clearly?

What is my profile as an artist?

Can you define your position in the art world? Have you never exhibited, only shown locally or do you consider yourself well-established? Have you largely shown in commercial, subsidised or public contexts? Has your work been reviewed locally, nationally or in specialist magazines? How are you regarded by other artists? If you were to approach galleries in which you are interested, would they have already seen your work or know your name?

In which part of the country do I want to exhibit?

Do you want to show close to home or further afield, within London, regionally or internationally?

Realistic expectations

By now, you should have built up a picture of yourself and your work. There may, however, be contradictions. You may want to communicate with the community but be shy about talking about your work. You might want to sell, but your work is relatively large and you haven't contacts with commercial galleries. Exhibiting may be important but you have little time to research and contact galleries. You'd like to tackle a gallery which shows established artists but you've got no exhibiting record. You may have big ambitions but dislike promoting yourself.

If any of these apply, you need to reassess your priorities. For example, if you have little time for promotion but great ambitions, you may have to be content with slower progress or decide to give your career greater priority in your life. If you want to sell you may need to change your format to make it saleable or accept that sales may only come about if you can find a suitable context. You might need to gain new skills in communication through formal training or by working with a community project, or you might need to attend a workshop to help you increase your presentation skills.

Research

Research means keeping well-informed about what is going on in your field in order to gain an awareness of the context in which you work. This may consist of looking at exhibitions in many galleries, seeing other artists' work, watching television and reading magazines and going to talks, seminars and conferences. Although the value of these things may not be immediately obvious, it is a way of storing up clues to your relationship to others and helps you place yourself in the context of the art world whilst at the same time giving you confidence to talk about issues related to your work.

At first, it might seem there is an overwhelming range of research sources, but in time, the selection of what is relevant to you becomes instinctive. A focused research strategy can lead to the opportunities you desire. For example, getting to know the characteristics of a magazine, who reviews for it and who is interested in work relating to yours, helps identify which writers might promote your career at some stage.

Researching galleries

The best way to get to know a gallery is to visit several times before trying to assess it, taking away printed information if there is any, looking at details of their other events and exhibitions and reading reviews of their shows. Be prepared to talk to gallery staff if the opportunity arises, asking pertinent questions and commenting on the show. For a broad picture of galleries in the UK and particularly those outside your locality, read the *Directory of Exhibition Spaces* which provides a thumbnail sketch of each venue. You could contact those you're interested in and get basic information. Check gallery listings for who's recently shown there and speak to artists concerned if possible. Read reviews and try to visit those which most appeal to you.

During a visit, it is useful to try to put into words the kind of work shown – figurative, abstract, issue-based, avant garde or traditional – and to assess the programme as a whole, working out what links it together, whether subject matter, issues or accessibility to a broad audience. Can you ascertain whether visitors are local, national or international; come from the art world or the community? Is it an art or non-art audience? Look at the profile of the exhibitors – are they young, unknown or established? What is the publicity like and does it attract reviews? Then, observe how the programme develops over a period of time and see whether the staff are approachable. Get used to making comparisons between galleries, assessing their relationship to one another and seeing whether your work fits in.

Making an informed choice

With so many galleries and opportunities how do you make a choice? This is where self-assessment and research come together. As galleries are looking for work which interests them and helps them fulfil their aims, so you must look for spaces which reflect your aims, interests and approach. If selling is a priority and you want to show quickly, a studio show might be best. However, if concerned with prestige and status you might decide to take time and approach established commercial galleries. If looking for somewhere to show installation, you might look at subsidised spaces, speak to independent curators or locate a space to set something up yourself. Those seeking to attract a wide audience and community involvement might seek out a school or a gallery with an education programme or even an alternative context like a launderette. If only interested in an art audience you will be looking for a gallery which not only attracts these people, but which also gets media coverage. If just starting out, have never shown or lack confidence, look for a local space – small commercial gallery, library space, arts centre, or café – whilst you learn the ropes without too much at stake.

If there is a significant gap between where you are at present and where you want to be in five years' time, you will need to approach galleries further up the hierarchy. If your idea of where you want to go seems to have links with other artists' career paths, you need to check how they made their way up by looking at their CVs and seeing where they have shown, if you know them ask their advice.

Creating opportunities

Although many artists perceive a lack of opportunities, there is, in fact, an infinite number available. If opportunities don't present themselves, you can create some for yourself. If you have an idea for a show but can't find a venue, why not organise an exhibition for yourself, get together with others to show, open your studios or organise discussions about how to work together to generate some more?

Make sure also that you don't let potential opportunities fall by the wayside. Don't miss inviting someone to the studio because you were taken aback by their interest. Did you turn down an opportunity because it wasn't exactly right? Would meeting another artist with similar ambitions make you think about collaborating? Would meeting an aspiring critic who likes your work lead to a way of fulfilling both your ambitions next time you show? Early in your career, it may be necessary to take opportunities which are not ideal in order to achieve something else. Alternatively, although you may know what you want, you may not be focusing on what you need to do to achieve it. For example, you may have identified galleries which could provide a stepping-stone to achieving your aims but have concentrated on others which were less intimidating.

If you are offered a show, prepare yourself by setting goals and working towards them. Every exhibition is an opportunity to realise ambitions and create further opportunities. Many artists put energy into making the work, framing it and hanging the show and then leave the exhibition and gallery to get on with it. Although this may work with a supportive and well-resourced gallery, many aren't in this position.

Action plan

Although an action plan sounds formal, it can simply be a written list or a set of things you need to think about at a particular time: for instance, before seeking an exhibition, when a show is planned or when you want to make changes in your career. Most artists with successful exhibiting careers do this in some way or another. If writing helps, make a list of aims and beside this, the actions you need to take to fulfil them.

London-based artist Cornelia Parker describes a plan she once used: "A couple of years out of college with little exhibiting experience, I'd built up a body of work which I wanted to show. I made a short-list of three galleries to approach, two of which were public." She chose galleries which interested her and which she felt might be sympathetic to her ideas. She carefully put together slides and outlined ideas for showing relevant to each venue. This brought one good exhibition opportunity which provided a catalyst for future shows. But years later when several successful shows had led to commissions, she began to feel uncomfortable. Some of the opportunities presenting themselves were not right for her or for the future development of her work. "Many of the proposed commissions were for the corporate world and more often than not based purely on the visual appearance of the work. For me, the ideas behind it were just as important: I didn't want to lose sight of that." She decided to turn down opportunities which would lead her further down the same path and take time to consider where she wanted to go with her work.

Self-investment

For most artists, costs of making are so great that few make a profit. However, it is important to invest in your work when necessary to achieve particular aims. Making but not showing can lead to isolation, disillusionment, or even stop you working. Investing in new equipment, going on a course to develop skills or updating your presentation needs to become essential to your practice.

Tundra Excavation, **ink on paper 210x185mm by** John Lancaster. **Photo:** the artist

One of a series of works arising from a studio visit to the Vesteralen region of northern Norway which was supported by South West Arts and Vesteralen Regionråd Kulturutvalget. An exhibition of the work was first shown at the International Arts Festival Norsk, Fiskeindustri-museum, before going to Brewery Arts, Cirencester.

Allocating time to self-promotion can also be a problem, as most artists have other jobs as well as domestic responsibilities. Many artists agree with Circencester-based artist John Lancaster that "a great deal of time and energy is needed to make contacts, organising slides, checking out exhibition spaces ... this time could be better spent (making art)...." Nevertheless, it is crucial to set aside enough time to do these things properly. To some extent, this means shifting your perception of what being an artist involves, and thinking about it as running a small business in which art making is only a part. Because it is important for artists to work consistently, taking time out for promotion and planning feels like stopping. But if you think of these areas as an integral part of the making process – rather like gathering source material for a new series of works – it won't seem quite so much of a chore to do it, and it will contribute to getting you where you want to be.

Isolation

As most opportunities arise from contact with others, isolation – caused by location or personal preference – is likely to work against you. But if geographical location is the problem, you can take positive steps to solve it: for example find out about other artists, activities or galleries in your vicinity by using regional and local resources like arts boards and arts councils. If you want to meet up with other artists with similar interests, try advertising in the local paper, in *Artists Newsletter*, or through local council or regional arts board newsletters. If new to an area, check out artists by going to open studios and arts festivals. City-based artists can feel isolated too. Ways of alleviating this include initiating meetings in each other's studios, inviting artists to see your work and participating in community-based activities. Take any opportunity to travel, see galleries and meet artists in other areas. Doing all these things should be recognised as an essential part of your work, giving you much-needed feedback and also widening your horizons.

Gaining confidence

Many artists lack confidence and even those who seem confident often lack self-esteem. For most, confidence waxes and wanes and even the most successful artists will probably experience times when their confidence is at a low ebb. Despite this, it is important to come across as confident when dealing with other professionals. Paul Hedge of Hayles Gallery confirms that an artist's confidence affects the way he feels about showing them. He needs to have confidence in them, not only because of the gallery's reputation but also because he works in the cafe and therefore tends to leave artists to mount their shows.

As there is strength in numbers, artists who lack confidence should make the most of their relationships with other artists by seeking feedback from them on their work and creating opportunities to talk about it. A more structured approach is taking assertiveness training or other courses to improve communication and presentation skills.

Being professional

Artists define professionalism variously as "taking my work seriously, and not compromising", "developing my career – getting stronger, better, farther", "earning a living from sales", "presenting myself and my work well", "skills and work well crafted"", "being businesslike –

keeping to deadlines, being methodical, reliable for others", "it's a question of commitment, dignity and self-respect." It means taking yourself and others seriously, presenting yourself well, being organised and well prepared for dealings with galleries; approaching appropriate galleries, having good documentation, keeping appointments, working to deadlines and fulfilling responsibilities. It also means having confidence in yourself and your work, knowing when to make an approach and being able to treat others as equal working partners. It involves negotiating and discussing difficulties or disputes with no loss of temper, and doing what you do to a high standard. A professional relationship begins with initial contact with a gallery and continues throughout the exhibiting process. Because as soon as you meet someone they begin to assess you, gallery directors observe that if you seem professional from the start, they are more likely to take you seriously.

Artists need not see their relationship with galleries as unequal, and taking control is important. For example, if you approach a gallery who shows interest in your work and says they'll get in touch, you could say you will telephone them instead and arrange a convenient time there and then to do so. Keep in mind that an exhibition is not a 'favour' to an artist nor is an artist doing the gallery a 'good turn'. It should be a mutually beneficial relationship.

It is tempting for an artist to imagine they are the only one with whom the gallery deals. Although their show is a priority as it draws near, for the gallery it is one of many. Demanding instant attention can work against you, and Duncan Smith of Central Space admits he turned down an artist who had constantly harassed him and with whom he couldn't face working.

Practising communication

Good communications skills are essential in developing professional relationships. Take every opportunity to talk and write about your work, whether casually with friends or more formally through giving talks or lectures. If opportunities don't arise, then create them yourself. Establish a group of artists which regularly meets to discuss art world issues or their work or invite people to your studio. Another way is to take a course which deals specifically with improving communication skills.

Making & developing contacts

Whilst many artists feel the art world is made up of those with contacts and those without, others positively hate the concept of using contacts to 'sell' themselves and get on, feeling it would undermine their independence and integrity. However, few artists achieve ambitions without contact with others and asking for or accepting help doesn't devalue talents, achievements or independence. Contacts include the well-known and the less-established, and as your career develops, so do the careers of your 'contacts' and you may end up being a 'contact' for them. Contacts begin with those you already know and your best contacts are other artists: for example, artists sit on selection panels, recommend other artists and curate shows. Many also initiate projects either independently or collaboratively with galleries, curators and organisations. Some artists move into writing, working for galleries or setting up their own and some go on to collect art. Rather than seeing the 'contacts' system as exclusive, you can accept it as another process which enables you to get where you want to be.

Students can begin making contacts at college, making the most of visiting lecturers and getting into the habit of visiting galleries and taking part in student shows. Contacts made then frequently lead to opportunities later and the nature of the contacts tends to dictate the opportunities which arise. Contacts after college are colleague artists, former tutors and those occasional lecturers as well as new people you meet. You can also take a more active approach by putting yourself into positions where you will meet like-minded people. For example, you can go to private views, gallery seminars, conferences or take a job in a gallery or arts organisation. Each time you are involved in an exhibition, arts project, gallery or university you inevitably meet others with whom you might generate new ideas.

It is valuable to get into the habit of following up any interest expressed, by inviting people to your studio and adding new names to your mailing list. An exhibition is the chance to follow up those contacts and maintain their enthusiasm for your work. Use it to invite other gallery directors, previous purchasers or commissioners and any writers you know. These small but well-planned actions will lead to a gradual development of career and reputation and, perhaps even to huge successes. As gallery director Maureen Paley says: "If someone turns you down, remember there is always someone else out there to help."

Time-scales & relationships

Many artists express frustration when they receive half a dozen rejections in a short period. But whilst some develop successful careers early on, for others success only follows many such disappointments, and it is maturity which may bring more appropriate opportunities. Some gallery directors like Francis Graham-Dixon believe that several years of consistent work makes an artist's work

Cold dark matter, **remains of exploded shed and contents suspended around a domestic lightbulb, by** Cornelia Parker.

more interesting. Independent curator Kay Roberts agrees: "I may know an artist's work for years before I am in a position to show it – the context has to be right for it." Alison Raftery of Matt's Gallery feels "it is a question of building up a dialogue between gallery and artist. This takes time and can't be forced. It depends on mutual interests, concerns and attitudes."

With a new body of work, an artist may be keen to show, but many galleries plan months – perhaps even years – in advance to organise, publicise and finance a show because its success depends on this. The build-up to an exhibition is also important for the artist, so work and ideas are resolved and plans are in place for making the most of the opportunity. Desperation can lead to mistakes or falling victim to the unscrupulous few who exploit such weakness by demanding too much or behaving dishonestly.

Developing a satisfying exhibiting career rarely happens overnight. It is more about social dialogue than formal procedures and even more about perseverance and planning than seeking instant success.

9 • Approaching galleries

Having established a short-list of galleries who are likely to find your work of interest, and that you and your work are ready to be put to the test, the next step is to plan the most effective way to approach them.

First, you have to know how and when to show them your work. The following information needs to be gathered either in person or over the telephone. Are they looking at new work now? Is there an up-coming deadline? To whom should material be sent and what exactly do they want to receive? Should the work be left to view and collected later, or will it be looked at while you wait? Their responses should be written down and kept safely! Also think if any contacts, other artists or colleagues could put in a good word for you, make an introduction to the director or, even better, show your slides or photographs to the gallery for you.

Whereas subsidised spaces tend to have defined procedures for looking at work, others may have ad-hoc viewings fitted in around other commitments. Slides may wait several months to be seen and may never be looked at unless you followup. Even if you get an appointment to take work in, it may be cancelled or postponed at the last minute when something more pressing comes up; looking at your work will not necessarily be a priority. If asked to telephone to arrange another time, then do so as perseverance may pay off. Whilst you shouldn't be easily put off, if you think you are wasting your time, look elsewhere. Getting a balance takes practice, so follow your instincts and learn from mistakes.

Telephone techniques

As first impressions are important, your first telephone call to a gallery needs careful planning. You need to decide how to begin the conversation and to compose what to say. If you are inexperienced, write down who you are, why you are ringing and the questions you want to ask. It makes you more confident and creates a good

External view of Godfrey & Twatt, Harrogate. Established in 1985, the gallery shows ceramics, original prints, jewellery, glass and wood and is on the Crafts Council's selected list. Work is selected mainly from established makers and artists "although we do take an interest in newcomers." As well as a continually changing stock, four or five exhibitions are held annually, these generally highlighting the work of an individual maker.

impression with the person on the other end. As all you want at this stage is information don't waste your time or theirs explaining yourself or your work. If you are following up someone who asked you to call them, or a contact suggested by someone else, it may take several calls before you get to talk to the right person, especially if the receptionist's job is to deflect incoming calls. But don't be put off if they seem unhelpful. If the person is not available, make it clear you were invited to make contact without exaggerating your relationship with the person for the sake of getting through. When you do get through, they may have forgotten you, so start off by reminding them, something on the lines of: "Hello, I'm Ahmed Khalid, we met last week at Hardware Gallery and you suggested I call you about my work." But these calls can be difficult to make, so pick a day when you feel confident. If you have to make a series of calls, begin with the one which least worries you, leading up to the most difficult as you gain confidence.

Making applications

Unless otherwise requested, an application should contain slides or photographs, statement about your work, CV and covering letter. You might include a catalogue from a previous show, especially if it was a solo show, and copies of good reviews. But don't include too much, it won't be looked at.

Curriculum vitae

For detailed information on preparing proposals and applications for exhibitions and other opportunities, see *Fundraising: the artist's guide to planning and financing work*, AN Publications.

This is basically a chronological list of information about you and your career. Every time you put one together, however, it must be geared towards the particular needs and interests of the organisation to whom you are applying. You may therefore have different versions for different situations and types of application. For example, if applying for an exhibition, previous exhibitions will be most important. If applying for a job, experience relevant to the position is more important. A CV generally includes:

• name
• home and/or studio address and contact telephone number
• place of birth and date if you want to give it
• qualifications if they are related to the application. Don't put your secondary school exam results though.

Other headings, to be selected according to particular situations, are:
• exhibitions – if you have enough, divide them into solo/two-person shows and group and mixed shows
• collections – public and private
• commissions – public and private
• awards
• bibliography – list exhibition reviews and catalogues
• broadcasting – list TV or radio items
• residencies.

Finally, you can include art-related work experience and any other information of interest to the particular application.

Inevitably, early in your career your CV will be short. Accentuate what you have done, for example perhaps you took part in a student show or showed work in a local café. If you've moved to an art career later in life some aspect of your previous work might be pertinent. Later on be more selective and taylor your CV to individual galleries: for example, a prestigious gallery may not be impressed by a library show, and a gallery with an education programme would be interested in previous contact with a local community. Ask more experienced artists to comment on your CV at draft stage and use their advice to perfect it.

Style and presentation of your CV are crucial. It should reflect you and make a good impression and ensure the person reading it can pick out the main elements. It must be typed on A4 paper with section headings in a bolder type or underlined. Traditionally, information was presented chronologically but nowadays, some artists follow the American method of putting most recent exhibitions and opportunities first. It is up to you which method you use. Use a standard format: dates on the left, title of exhibition, whether solo, group etc, gallery name, place, if abroad country too. Similarly, give award title and who gave it, name of publication for reviews or catalogues, author and issue number and date. If your CV is being used outside the UK, check usual formats for the country concerned and whether you need to get it translated.

If good at writing, you can include a short paragraph about yourself and your work at the beginning. Some artists include a photocopied photograph of a piece of work or themselves although this may not always elicit the desired response if the image isn't of good quality or your portrait does not exude confidence. Something visual attracts attention and can alleviate potential boredom: a human touch can make a difference.

Remember, however, that a CV is backup to documentation rather than of immense importance. It must set a scene and encourage the reader to seek more information.

Writing about your work
Many artists find it difficult to write about their work. Things which come intuitively in images are often difficult to put into words and some artists feel the work should 'speak for itself.' However, since most people tend to communicate verbally, it is important to be able to write about your work and reduce the potential problems of other people 'interpreting' it for you!

Start by asking yourself, "To whom is my statement directed and what would they want to know?" What you include depends on a combination of what your work is about, the nature of the exhibition you are applying for and the venue's aims and programme. Keep the writing straightforward and concise. Don't use jargon or abbreviations and don't repeat yourself. One side of an A4 sheet of paper is generally enough.

Make initial notes based on what your work is about; your answers to self-assessment questions in **8 • Self-assessment** will help this process. Enlarge the notes first into sentences and then paragraphs, each covering a particular topic or point. Avoid repeating words – use a thesaurus for another word with the same meaning. Make the statement 'flow', with each sentence following from the last in a natural progression. When you have made your best attempt ask a friend or another artist to read it and incorporate their advice into a final draft.

1993: a teenage girl is raped repeatedly, scrubbed all over with a wire brush, set alight and left to burn: she died later in hospital **by** Sophie Boddington **from the 'Hear no evil' series of posters exhibited in Soho, London in April 1994.**

These were first exhibited in a student show at Marks & Spencers' London offices but were taken down almost immediately, "because people there seemed unwilling to be confronted with the issues raised. We are all so dead to the words printed on the pages of newspapers or spoken by television news readers. I believe we have an ability to remove ourselves from these words as though reading a story or watching a film. By making these drawings, I not only experienced a cathartic process and rid myself of some of the guilt and shame I felt at being unable to prevent such atrocities, but I was also able to make people think about our 'Hear no evil, see no evil' attitude. If seeing my work makes one person think for a moment about their human relationship to victims and perpetrators of the crimes depicted, then the work has been worthwhile."

Application forms

As some situations require you to fill in an application form, it's important to do this clearly and provide all information requested. Start off by reading the conditions carefully to see if your work is eligible or whether other conditions would exclude you from applying. As you read, note actions you must take, for example "deliver your work to ..." or "attach label to back of work." Answer all sections precisely but fully. Try out on a photocopy first and make sure the final application is legible and looks professional. Don't send information not asked for.

Covering letter

With the exception of application forms, always send a covering letter which is brief and to the point. If you've already met and talked to the person to whom your letter is addressed, remind them of this and who you are. If you have been recommended to approach them by someone else, say who that person is. Always say why you are contacting them, that is, you would like to be considered for an exhibition. List material sent as a record for them and you, and keep a copy of the letter. Enclose a stamped addressed envelope for the return of material.

Visual documentation

Good visual documentation of previous work is the starting point for all new projects and applications. It may be the first impression a gallery or curator has of your work. Photographs may also be used by the media, and not having good images at the right time may mean lost opportunities. Keeping up-to-date and good-quality documentation should become an integral part of an artist's practice, but if your camera skills are shaky, you may be better off paying a professional to take your slides until you have time to improve.

Most galleries look at 35mm slides, although It is becoming more common for artists to make colour prints, but before you send them check with the gallery. Note that slides have to be in focus, correctly lit and show nothing other than your work. Colour prints can be made from slides as can colour laser print copies. The art press can usually handle colour slides and black and white prints, although the former are invaluable for printed publicity material for an exhibition as well as for colour postcards. Black and white prints can be used as press photographs, for use with proposals, and for catalogues and other printed publicity at smaller venues who can't afford colour printing.

If you make installation or time-based work, different problems arise. Still photography may be used to suggest sequential imagery or an environment, but you might want to try using a video camera. The results may have more impact and an increasing number of venues have facilities for playback.

Selecting slides

When selecting images to go with an application, don't send too many slides. An experienced viewer can gain a good idea from six or eight, and quickly assess whether your work is suitable for them. If sending slides through the post, use glassless mounts, but not cardboard which sticks in projectors. Send them in a flat plastic slide sheet available from photographic shops rather than in boxes or a pile taped together. Spend time arranging the sheet so that the set looks interesting and explanatory, each image relating to those around it. Studio shots suggest scale and details give a feeling of materials or texture. Never include images which are not relevant to that particular application. Choose slides which have the truest colour and which have the same light temperature, that is, ensure that a white wall is the same colour white in each shot. If your work is not square in the frame, adjust it in the mount. Label each slide with at least your name and 'top' and add title, medium, date and dimensions if possible, using slide labels from a photographic shop. Always include these details on a separate sheet which also has your name on as this can be read while slides are projected.

Presenting photographs

Photographs are best mounted on card or placed in a bound book with transparent sleeves don't just send a pile with the same advice for putting them in order as for slides. Start and finish with something strong and memorable. Label each image with relevant details, obviously ensuring labels don't partially obscure images. You can also make a title page and include your statement in one sleeve. The layout should be consistent for each page; a change in size of print can detract from the overall feeling.

If a gallery approaches you

For an explanation of legal terms and sample exhibition contracts, see *NAA Public Exhibition Contract*, AN Publications

Sometimes galleries approach artists, on recommendation or because they've seen your work elsewhere. Although this sounds an ideal situation, don't rush into accepting an offer straight away. Arrange a time to meet and, at the meeting, keep calm and ask the same questions you would if you were making an approach. For instance, how the gallery is run and what the financial and practical arrangements would be. If they won't answer in a straightforward way, it is fair to be cautious. If you've never been to the gallery, visit and check it out. Ask who else has shown and if you know any of the artists, try to get to speak to some of them. Check out media coverage and reviews, ask to see catalogues and publicity from previous shows. Ask to see a copy of the gallery's exhibition contract if they have one. Never commit yourself without fully understanding terms, and never leave work without a receipt.

Interviews & studio visits

At various stages in developing relationships with galleries, you are likely to be asked to go and show them your work, either through an interview, taking in a portfolio or giving a presentation of a particular proposal. Whatever form it takes, your folio or documentation needs to be well-organised and presented in a professional and interesting way. Photographs need to be mounted on board, and art works carefully selected to create the desired impression. Careful planning will ensure you have got the order right and have anticipated all likely questions. If in doubt, test it out on another artist, ex-tutor or friendly gallery director friend.

Allow plenty of time for the appointment and be sure to arrive on time. If late, you may find another artist has been given your slot or the gallery director has left for an appointment elsewhere. On the other hand, be prepared to wait a while if the director is running late. Whilst trying to keep your main aim in mind – to put over your work well – respond carefully to questions, and if you feel you haven't said important things, attempt to direct the interview so you have the chance to do so. If at the end you haven't had a definite response, you may have to ask a direct question. Be prepared for it to go either way or to still not get a clear 'yes' or 'no'. Try nevertheless to assess how it has gone and whether there is an interest. If a director says, "I like what I've seen but can't offer you anything at the moment, so keep in touch", they may mean it, so it's up to you to follow up later. But if the response is more vague, you'll have to gauge whether it's worth pursuing against any other potential opportunities. If you are turned down, ask if they can suggest another gallery more appropriate for your work as this helps you build contacts and you may find what you are looking for elsewhere.

Studio visits

Gallery directors often make brief exploratory visits to studios, so you have to make the best of a small amount of time to make a good impression. Prepare yourself by trying to visualise your work in their gallery. Although it may be difficult in a small studio, create at least one

Museum Piece **by** Frederick Bell**, 1992, has nine inter-related parts derived from site-specific works installed in a Victorian museum. The initial works were installed in a glass display case and refer to issues raised by the contents of an identical case just across the gallery.**

'The Deconstructed Image', showing work by Frederick Bell, Pierre Antoine, Heinz Cibulka and Marc Schepers was a collaboration between Angel Row Gallery, Nottingham and Galerie Ruimte Morguen, Antwerp and aimed to challenge perceptions of imagery, both physically and ideologically, allowing a re-interpretation of the propositions made by and through photographs.

clear wall (painting it if necessary), against which to present work. Organise works you want to show so they are easily accessible, especially if you only have space to show one at a time. If you work at home, consider how to make the room you use as a studio or another room look like a professional's space. Keep your domestic life in the background, with children and animals out of sight so you can concentrate.

Perhaps surprisingly, it is often both gallery director and artist who feel nervous of what the director of a major public gallery describes as "a strange experience. You walk into the studio of someone you may hardly know and strike up an intimate conversation about their work." There may be a feeling of pressure to make comments or judgements. It can be difficult if the work is not suitable for the programme or the person concerned doesn't like the work. Any indication of interest may lead to the artist expecting to get a show when in reality, it may not be possible for the foreseeable future. Some directors admit they dislike having to impart bad news to artists. Ways to make the situation more relaxed include offering a seat and tea or coffee; and if they sit, sit down yourself.

Talking about your work

There is a balance to be found between having too little to say and saying too much. Aim to be responsive, listen carefully to what they say and any questions asked, trying to answer briefly but fully and at the same time keeping in mind what you wanted to say about your work. Don't, however, try to explain everything or take them on a 'tour' of all your recent thoughts as this could be overwhelming. It's a good idea to have a couple of questions to ask them, as this indicates your interest in the gallery and potential relationship with it. Talking about work is often difficult, and inevitably most artists feel a little nervous when confronted with a director whose decision can affect their future. But, taking it philosophically, remember that if this gallery doesn't take your work another opportunity will arise.

Rejection

Inevitably, dealing with rejection is hard, especially in the early years when it feels you're never going to get anywhere. But rejection isn't necessarily tied to quality. It may be your work doesn't fit the programme or that they've had several similar applications and simply chose someone else's. Most galleries don't give reasons, but if you felt sure your work was right for the space, you made a good presentation and felt rapport with gallery staff, try asking for feedback. You may not get it – so weigh up the value before asking. If interest was expressed in spite of rejection, follow up say a year later, and perseverance and maturity may pay off.

Getting used to the ups and downs of an artist's career may make rejection easier to cope with, and although it always hurts it is possible to learn to put it in context, and to move on with confidence to the next opportunity.

10 • Making an exhibition work

The offer of a show is the beginning of a complex and sometimes lengthy process and since many shows are offered up to 18 months in advance, think about how best to use the opportunity. Making the work or developing ideas for an installation can be woven into the preparatory work needed for promotion, education or other events. The process may involve many discussions and meetings.

It is important to discuss the nature of the relationship with the gallery and clarify early on who is responsible for publicity and promotion, selecting and hanging work, transport and framing, selling and organising the private view and other events. Your research and contact with the gallery will have given you a good idea of what they take on and a contract can confirm the details. However, many galleries operate on a less formal basis and don't use contracts, and this may lead to disagreements if things don't get done or gallery and artist have different expectations. If there are any areas of responsibility you are unsure of, phone to discuss the issue with them. Even if the gallery doesn't provide a contract, you can put the outcome of your discussions with them in writing. At the very least ask for written confirmation of the exhibition offer.

See also NAA Public Exhibition Contract, Richard Padwick, AN Publications, for information on exhibition contracts.

How much you have to do depends on the nature of the gallery. A library space will probably leave most of the work to you, and whereas a commercial gallery charging 50% commission should take most of the responsibility, you may still collaborate on promotion by going to media interviews or contributing personal contacts. A plan of action is useful and this chapter looks at ways of making the exhibition work for you. Your questions on self-assessment will help identify what is appropriate to your exhibition.

Promotion

Promotion is an ongoing part of an artist's working life and an exhibition is an ideal opportunity to make extra efforts to further your ambitions. This may include seeking media coverage, organising promotional events, targeting publicity to relevant people, making contact with other galleries, approaching potential buyers, commissioners or others who might take an interest. Promotion should be specific to you, your work and the gallery.

You need to establish responsibilities between you, the other exhibitors and the gallery and be aware of who is dealing with promotion. If you have specific ambitions and ideas about how to promote the show, or broaden audiences for your work, discuss these early on with the gallery and/or the other artists involved. Take an active part in how your show works. Pooling resources, contacts and ideas will enhance your chances of creating further opportunities. An ambitious gallery will be as keen as you, but it is surprising how many do not think ahead in this way. If they are not bothered take the initiative yourself and enlist the help of contacts and friends.

Getting media interest

The method of attracting media interest depends on whether the show is group or solo, the type of gallery, the resources available, your relationship with the gallery and your combined contacts. Having discovered what the gallery can do, your role is to come up with ways of filling the gaps. A review is most artists' and galleries' ideal promotion, but with so many exhibitions to choose from it can be difficult to attain. Even though invitations go out, most media people only come if they know the artist or the gallery, or if the exhibition links with their interests or those of their editors. Part of the follow-up is to telephone key people who didn't come and to give them a reason to do so: offer a personal tour, tell them about an evening lecture with refreshments, lunchtime art press view, etc. But make sure the gallery is happy to host such things, and it is even better if the director is there too.

Advertising

Paid for advertising in specialist magazines is good, not just for getting audience, but for promoting your name to people who won't get to see the show. This is all good for a burgeoning reputation, but it can be expensive. The gallery may pay, but if not, try sharing the costs with the gallery and/ or other exhibitors.

Printed publicity

Printed publicity may include invitations, posters, leaflets and catalogue. Invitations are a basic necessity. A personal invitation is the best way to persuade people to come. If the gallery handles the printing and distribution of them, get some for your own use. A personal handwritten note with a card can make someone feel particularly welcome.

A catalogue can be impressive promotional tool used to attract the attention of press and media, potential buyers and other galleries. If the gallery can't afford to produce one, can you and the other artists involved help pay for it. A professional looking catalogue can go on working for you many years after the exhibition.

The show is up

Although you've realised your ambition, and the show is up, the sense of achievement is often accompanied by a feeling of anticlimax, exhaustion and sometimes depression. Whilst group or mixed shows are often described as being 'more fun' for the artists, private views for solo shows are more stressful as there's more at stake. Some artists deal with the aftermath by taking a little time off, picking up other aspects of their lives, seeking other activities and some go straight back to work. Notwithstanding this, you have to make the best of the show whilst it's up, using it to build contacts and credibility and also to create new opportunities.

Pursuing exhibitions

If you have ambitions to make showing an important part of your practice, this is an ideal time to pursue them. Gallery directors and the media are more likely to see a show than visit your studio. The exhibition is an opportunity to widen your audience and make contacts, especially if you have some in hand to follow up. Discussions with the gallery should have established what kind of promotion it does during the show, and this might include inviting potential clients to look with a view to buying, contacting press and media and inviting others who can offer opportunities.

A well-resourced and supportive gallery may handle all these things. However, it is frequently surprising to artists how many galleries don't followup on their shows and if the artist plays no part in this either, the opportunity may be wasted.

To ensure it isn't, after a few days away from it, assess the situation. Think over what happened at the private view and who you met. Make a list of any offers or suggestions made and the things you need to follow up. For example, someone may have said they would like to come back to see the show with you at more leisure. Next, make a list of people – gallery directors, other artists, colleagues, etc – you invited who didn't come and consider ways of encouraging them to come whilst the show's up. Check back to the aims you identified before the show was up and look again at the best way of achieving them, whether by contacting particular people, sending slides or following up leads for reviews, etc.

Inevitably, you will find the list can be divided into things you feel confident about doing, those you feel doubtful about and others you really feel you can't do single-handed. Having completed your list, make a timetable of days on which you will telephone people, send out photographs, catalogues, etc. Start with the aspects you feel confident about as the first few calls will probably be difficult, but it gets easier as you gain confidence. The follow-up which you feel unable to make could perhaps be done by colleague artists or the gallery director who can smooth the way for you whilst also endorsing your work.

If the gallery is equally willing to maximise the outcome of the exhibition, as soon as you have drawn up your action list, talk it through with them, check it against their plans and perhaps tasks can be shared between you. Bear in mind that how much the gallery can do depends on their aims and resources.

Approaching other galleries

If you want to make showing an important part of your practice, think ahead and use your show to attract other opportunities. You may have ideas and contacts, but ask the gallery for advice and discuss the best way to approach others – eg send out catalogues, offer a tour, negotiate a collaborative event. Target relevant places as you did when seeking this show and if the gallery can make the approach for you, so much the better.

A commercial or private gallery which has taken responsibility for organisation and costs may take control of this promotional work, especially if they are interested in developing a regular relationship with you, but still welcome your ideas and contacts. Although some galleries may be against you making contacts with other commercial galleries (where a conflict of interest is perceived), approaching a public space will usually be seen as mutually beneficial. Most subsidised galleries accept your need to approach other galleries and are often willing to help.

The private view

The private view is probably the most important promotional event of the show as well as being a social occasion. Whilst private views for group or mixed shows are often described as 'more fun', for solo shows there's more at stake and it can be stressful. As the artist in the spotlight, you are still at work and it is essential to make the most of the opportunity to welcome your quests, meet people the gallery invites and discuss your work with those who might provide further opportunities. If the promotion has worked well and attracted a significant attendance, you may have to work hard throughout the evening, particularly if it is a solo show.

A supportive gallery should introduce you to relevant people, but if they don't get out there and do it for yourself. If it is a group show arrange with other artists to introduce each other to quests. Most people will respect your need to make new contacts and talk to different people and you will need to develop the social skills necessary to achieve a good balance between spending time with your friends and talking to others.

What if things go wrong

The exhibition process can be complex, involving a wide range of activities, issues and personalities and it is rare for the whole process to go smoothly from start to finish – mistakes may be made, important things forgotten and when people are under pressure to complete work to deadlines, disagreements can arise and tempers can be lost.

See also *NAA Public Exhibition Contract*, Richard Padwick, AN Publications, for information exhibition contracts.

Many of these hiccups are resolved as they arise, but handling them can be difficult for artists and exhibition organisers alike. Developing the skills to communicate and negotiate are the artist's best approach to difficulties and disputes. Keep calm, find out as much as you can about what has happened. If you are unhappy, take time to think through your viewpoint and discuss it with another artist, before taking the matter up with the person concerned. If you have a contract or letter of agreement which covers the issue, refer to it. The aim is to find a solution acceptable to both parties so that the exhibition process can go ahead.

Although the majority of shows offered are followed through to conclusion, some fall through. This has become common during the recession and can happen at any stage in the exhibiting process. The gallery may run out of funds – perhaps a sponsorship deal has fallen through and the exhibition programme has to be revised. Some close down altogether cancelling all future shows. Other examples include: the exhibition organiser who chose the artist leaves and the new organiser won't honour the previous arrangement; the gallery director has a change of mind as doubts about the work creep in; too many shows have been selected for the programme and one has to be postponed.

The cancellation of an exhibition is always upsetting for the artist. Many experienced artists take the attitude that a show is never definite until the work is on the wall. In most cases there is little you can do; however if you have spent money, for example on framing work, you may have a right to compensation. Try to negotiate and put your point of view without losing your temper. If your contract covers cancellation, refer to this. It is important to recognise that whilst a contract is technically enforceable it may prove too expensive and time-consuming to use the courts to seek redress.

Private galleries are not regulated in any way; however a gallery receiving public funds is, to some extent, accountable to the funder. If you feel you have been treated badly, you could inform the funding body. This may not help you directly, but the funding body may raise the issue as a matter of principle when they carry out their assessment of the gallery for future funding. This contributes to the empowerment of artists since, if one complaint has no effect, a dozen from different artists must be taken more seriously.

Selling work

If selling work is important, you need to have a clear strategy about how best to approach it. As the majority of sales take place at the private view, it is crucial to prepare for this possibility. If selling work is your responsibility, make it obvious that work is for sale by establishing sale prices in advance and putting a price list in a prominent place. On the practical side, you'll need a packet of red dots to be stuck on sold works, a receipt book and/or sales agreement to record the details of a sale. Be prepared for the various methods of payment – cheque, cash and credit card – and decide what you will do if someone wants to pay in instalments. If sales are handled by the gallery, refer buyers to the relevant person and don't in any way undermine an agreement made with the gallery.

Ideally, selling is a collaborative effort. Even if the gallery does take this on, if you know potential buyers, people who have previously bought from you or expressed an interest in doing so, or even relevant

See also Organising your exhibition, Debbie Duffin, AN Publications, for information about the practicalities of selling

See also 2 •
Galleries &
exhibition spaces
and 8 • Education &
interpretation

public collections, let the gallery know. If they didn't come to the private view, a call from you or gallery may encourage them to do so. There can be problems if the gallery takes responsibility for sales but isn't good at dealing with potential customers. Be aware of what is going on. For example, if someone keeps coming back to look at a particular piece, they are obviously tempted and the person handling sales should respond by striking up a conversation, discovering their level of interest, why they are hesitating. Their job is to encourage them to make a purchase. If you see opportunities being missed because the gallery is not trying to sell, you might intervene. Ways of dealing with it depend upon your relationship with the gallery, whether you feel confident to deal with the potential buyer and if you think you can gently prod gallery staff into action. It could be, for example, that diplomatically engineering a discussion between customer and gallery staff provides the solution.

Documentation

An exhibition in which your work is presented to its best advantage, with clean walls and good lighting, is an ideal time to document individual pieces as well as the show overall. It is advisable to take 35mm slides and black and white prints, and using two cameras makes this easier. Take them early on so you see the results before the show comes down and you can take more if they aren't good enough.

Good documentation undoubtedly helps your career. Apart from general use with future applications, it can be used to make the most of the exhibition whilst it is on. For example, if a review is proposed and you have good prints easily available, your work may be printed. Prompt response to a media request for visuals may mean your work rather than anyone else's is illustrated with a review of a group show.

Although some galleries organise the taking of photographs to send to the media, not all do and you may have to supply them. Ideally, photographs for press use should be available at the private view, especially if you anticipate media interest, as many publications work to tight schedules and can't wait for prints.

Assessing your work

Simon Edmondson who shows with the Benjamin Rhodes Gallery working in his ACME studio which was open to the public during the 1994 Whitechapel Open exhibition. Photo: *ACME*

Most artists feel their own assessment of a show is the most important and the views of others they respect – gallery, reviewers, other artists and friends – are important. Once the show is up, there is time to look at it objectively. The artist can assess whether s/he is happy with it, in what ways it could have been better, what changes s/he would make in future and to consider how presentation to the public will affect the work's development. It's also an ideal opportunity to listen to other people's views. Although this begins at the private view, it can continue if you actively seek conversations – with artists and others whose opinions you respect – about what you have done and your new ideas. If the gallery isn't doing it, you might even arrange specific events to generate critical discussion, checking first that the gallery won't find such initiatives a problem.

Broadening audiences

As an increasing number of galleries in the subsidised sector run education programmes linked to exhibitions you may be interested in being involved during your exhibition. You might choose to do so to broaden your audience and encourage more visitors to your exhibition or to gain satisfaction from passing on technical skills or knowledge and understanding of contemporary or historical art. Working with a gallery education programme not only generates income but can also help you develop ideas and skills, get new perspectives on your work and engage the interest of those who might offer you opportunities in future.

You might be involved in doing seminars, lectures, workshops for specific groups of people or in doing guided tours for gallery visitors. In some cases, artists do gallery residencies in which they work with children or other groups to bring an exhibition to life and give insight into contemporary practices. Artists necessarily have different levels of interest in such work and, because they need to be skilled communicators to do it, may not always find it suitable for them. But if this is an area in which you wish to gain experience and the gallery doesn't run any kind of programme, you could take the initiative and organise something yourself, having first asked yourself the following questions:

- Do I have the necessary skills or enthusiasm to learn them?
- Do I enjoy working with people?
- With which groups of people would I like to work? (For example children, adults, people with disabilities, etc.)
- Is my work suitable to use in this context?
- Am I free at the times when these people would want what I have to offer?

Lectures

As giving a lecture may involve standing up in front of a crowd of people and talking about your work either with or without accompanying slides, successful delivery depends on being confident about whether you can express ideas clearly and in a way appropriate to specific audiences. Even if you don't read from your notes when you actually give a lecture, it is advisable to write down what you intend to say and where the slides fit in to check whether you have included all your main points and that the talk will fit the time allocated. As a dummy run, you can either talk yourself through the lecture, or better still try it out

Clay wall relief by Ranjit Kaur Dhanjal **from 'Crafts from a Golden Tradition' a Craftspace Touring exhibition shown at Wednesbury Art Gallery as part of the 1993 South Asian Arts Festival as the first of a twelve-venue tour. Photo:** *Ming de Nasty*

Researched by artist Ranbir Babrah, the exhibition provides an opportunity to show work for 13 Asian women whose experience and learning lies outside the British design education system. Craftspace Touring promotes understanding of and access to high-quality contemporary crafts through exhibitions and touring events, and this exhibition forms part of a series concerned with developing cultural diversity in the crafts.

on someone else. As you gain experience you may just rely on notes or the slides themselves to prompt you. Slides need to be good quality with a clear link between images and what you say.

Organise slides either in a carousel or in a way which makes them easy to transfer to one. In the latter case, allow time when you arrive at the lecture to do this. If you are unsure about using a projector, spend a little time trying it out before the audience comes in. Ensure also that there is sufficient light to see your notes or other reference material whilst you are speaking. As time is usually allocated for questions afterwards, it's a good idea to end by inviting questions or asking the audience a question. Be aware, however, that audiences are unpredictable, with some responding immediately and others taking a considerable time to warm up. For a first lecture, it helps to prime someone from the gallery or lecture venue to start the ball rolling, as this encourages others to join in.

Talks

As talks and guided tours are generally less formal than lectures they require a broader range of communication skills. You may be physically closer to the audience and more involved with them; this means a talk may be punctuated with questions and responses. Although some artists find this easier to cope with as there is more input from the audience, others find it more difficult since it can lead off on a tangent from an original structure and generate unexpected responses. However, you are quite entitled to throw a question back or admit you can't answer and ask whether anyone else can help. Another tactic is to comment that this is an interesting point which you'd like to return to later – when you've had time to think about it a little more! Rather than making you look a fool, such strategies are more likely to endear you to your audience and put them at ease.

A talk may also be billed as a seminar, in which the object is to generate discussion in a structured way. Some seminars involve a group of speakers and a chairperson to facilitate proceedings and invite the audience to participate.

Workshops

Gallery workshops are interactive affairs in which artists guide participants through various thought processes and practical steps to arrive at a specific end. Running a workshop demands a complex balance of skills as artists need to be good at listening and imparting information and concepts and also be able to manage a group of people by encouraging those who are attentive and controlling those who are overbearing. Workshops with children and young people require an extra ability to keep discipline without losing flexibility and creativity.

The best workshops happen when an artist's interests and skills are the focus for a workshop topic. For example, a painter dealing with sociopolitical images might plan a workshop around these themes and their particular painting skills. Artists who are inexperienced are not advised to 'learn on the job' however, but to find ways of working alongside a more experienced artist. Some structured courses are run to help artists gain skills for working in educational settings; these are generally advertised in magazines like *Artists Newsletter* or in other regional newsletters.

Taking the initiative

If you'd like to do some educational work and the gallery doesn't run an education programme, you could still discuss your ideas with them – preferably well in advance of the exhibition – and set out to initiate some events yourself by using your contacts. For example, you may know a lecturer at a college who would bring a group of students or have contact with a school which might like a workshop. Spend time listening to their needs and look for links with your work, interests and skills. If you are suggesting something more complex than a straightforward talk, you will need to put a proposal to them which demonstrates how your needs and theirs coincide and describes costs and practicalities involved. If they are interested, it can be planned in more detail and the necessary funds raised or organised from the host.

For detailed information on preparing proposals and raising funds for visual arts projects, see Fundraising: the artist's guide to planning and financing work, AN Publications

After the show is over ...

Once the show has come down, there are still things to be done. It may be your responsibility to transport work back to the studio, deliver sold works or chase up those who have yet to pay in full. Keep your relationships good with all people who've helped – gallery, sponsors or funding bodies, artists and other supporters – by thanking them in person or by letter. And keep pegging away at any other possibilities, for example that gallery which suddenly showed an interest in the last few days or someone you met with whom you developed a rapport.

Last but not least, congratulate yourself. Doing an exhibition is hard work and you have probably learned a great deal. You've done what you set out to do, and even if you haven't achieved your highest hopes, you've widened your audience, consolidated your reputation and made new contacts. There are also likely to be other spin-offs which may not immediately be obvious. Sometimes years later, a curator or collector may remember your work and get in touch, or an art magazine review read long after the event may generate a commission, some teaching or another show.

11 • Evaluating the experience

Finding out what others thought of your exhibition is one form of assessment, and discussing the work with friends, other artists, gallery staff and visitors all helps. Consider comments in the visitors' book and re-read any reviews or a catalogue essay, using these responses to compare your views with those of others. However, you can embark on a more systematic approach, by asking yourself the following questions.

What did you achieve?
This could be a list including new opportunities, new contacts, new skills acquired, interesting responses, media coverage and sales of work.

Were these things you had hoped for or planned or did they happened unexpectedly?

How did they come about?
This could be a description of what actions were taken and by whom.

Which aims weren't fulfilled and why?
For example, did you or the gallery neglect to do something, were your expectations too high or inappropriate for the context? Perhaps you didn't set goals, or maybe your aims have changed and you weren't prepared for new things to happen.

How can you build on this for the future?
Perhaps opportunities arose, contacts were made and ideas were developed which could be followed up or dealt with later on.

What would you like to achieve next time you show and what actions would you take to achieve them?
The experience of this show should have given you valuable information to be used next time you exhibit. Writing down key points so that they can be referred to is a more effective way of retaining the information than trying to hold it in your head.

Mixed Company, **28" x 40" pastel drawing by** Linda Cooper. **Photo:** the artist

Isis Gallery, a small private space in rural Cumbria run by artist Irene Faith, shows emerging and established artists mainly from the North of England. With a sympathetic approach to installation and multi-disciplinary practitioners it also provides opportunities for artists to produce site-specific or location-based works.

Starting work again

Whereas some artists begin work again fairly soon after the show, often within days, either because they are encouraged by the experience and the ideas it has thrown up or because they have another show or opportunity for which to work, others find it more difficult. Although the smoothest path back into work is achieved by those who work consistently whatever the circumstances, not all can do this. Some use the natural break from the studio caused by an exhibition as a moment to stop and think, have a break to replenish themselves, or to pursue related activities like promotion or documentation.

Continuing gallery relationships

There are many ways in which artists may continue or develop their relationship with a particular gallery. In the subsidised sector for example, this might be through education projects or inclusion in a group show. You might be asked to recommend other artists to exhibit or there may be opportunities to initiate projects with them in the future. Commercial galleries are more likely to seek a regular and formalised relationship with artists they show and tend to have vested interests in a mutually exclusive agreement, especially if your show was a commercial success.

If you are offered an exclusive contract though, take time and advice from others to ascertain whether this would be good for you at this particular time and with this particular gallery. Although it may seem that the gallery has control over the nature of the relationship, it isn't necessarily the case, and you should not be shy of making a decision about whether you want to continue it and in what way. Galleries, like artists, develop and change, and many are open to suggestion.

You might, however, feel the experience wasn't a good one and not want to continue the relationship. But try to assess the situation dispassionately, especially if the gallery has indicated a desire to show your work again. It may have been that there were conflicting experiences: some things went wrong but at the same time you made sales. In such cases, weigh up the pluses and minuses carefully and in doing this, it helps to take advice from more experienced artists. If a mutually beneficial relationship develops, it may continue happily for years. Even so, it is still important to remain aware of what you want from the situation, and if things change, that you feel fully consulted and happy with what is happening to you.

What next?

Artists' careers develop over a period of time, sometimes with big steps but more often through a series of small steps taking them nearer to their goals, or through a subtle set of changes of direction. Each exhibition is just one opportunity in a series which makes up your career. Having assessed the success of your exhibition, absorbed its lessons and recovered from fatigue, it is time to begin to look at what next. You next step may relate to the positive things which happened and/or ways you want the experience to be different next time and answers to the above questions will provide the clues.

Questions asked in **8 • Self-assessment** can also help. This time round though, you have more experience, the advantage of seeing the outcome of your actions, greater knowledge of your strengths and weaknesses. You are more capable of being assertive and if things go wrong, in a stronger position to make informed decisions. Perhaps now you are thinking about a different type of gallery, new context or a different set of goals, or even of embarking on some entirely new ways of working. If it was your first exhibition, you may want to try something completely different to provide yourself with a range of experiences from which to choose directions for the future.

If you try one way over a period of time and it doesn't work, stop and ask yourself whether this is right for you. Later on though, decisions can be made on the basis of past achievements. For example, if you've had several shows in local libraries and been in a couple of local mixed exhibitions, you might now approach a small gallery for a solo show, or a more prestigious one with an idea for a group show with others in your studio. If you've shown quite widely in 'alternative' venues in London, you might want to approach prestigious regional galleries which might include you in a group show. If you've shown widely outside London, you may think the time right to approach London venues. On the other hand, if you've been reasonable successful with a small commercial gallery, you might want to look to moving up to a more prestigious one which can promote you better.

Equally important is to keep in mind your broader aims and ambitions and to direct your choices towards achieving them. For instance, if you are looking towards showing in major regional galleries and there are many to choose from, each with different reputations and links with others, you need to determine which would be most likely to provide the stepping stone you need. But whenever you consider making a leap, refer back to **8 • Self-assessment**. Even if you develop a reputation which opens doors, what you gain will still be related to the match between you and gallery.

There might be specific things you didn't achieve for which you would like to aim in future. For example, if you hoped for a review which didn't happen, check out what you should do to make it more likely next time. If there are things you know will help you achieve your goals, you may decide the best way is to take control of them yourself.

Developing a context

A context may mean the type of venue in which your work is seen, for example, the commercial sector or public art arena, but it also means how your work relates to that of other artists, to historical or contemporary traditions and to critical concerns. Developing a context helps in pursuing ambitions and in gaining interest and recognition from those who might help, and also assists others to gain access to your work.

Developing the context can be achieved in different ways, the first step being to identify the links described above. Answers to the questions in **8 • Self-assessment** help to do that. An understanding of the context can be applied when seeking new exhibitions. For example, if you are thinking about broadening your audience through a group show, be selective and choose to show with artists with whom you have something in common – links between work, common ambitions or the desire to attract a similar audience. In this way, you

For the Pot, **charcoal on paper, 1988 by** Kim Tong **from 'Reclaiming the Madonna: artists as mothers'. Organised by Usher Gallery, Lincoln and curated by Janita Elton and Susan Wilson, the exhibition addresses the issue of how motherhood affects female creativity. Selected by both invitation and open submission, it contains work by 30 artists including Eileen Cooper, Sandra Fisher, Sarah Raphael and Laetitia Yhap and includes installation, photography, illustration, drawing, painting, printmaking and sculpture. Seminars and workshops which continue the debate accompany each showing in the six-venue tour until February 1995.**

will generate a coherent show with promotion geared towards a specific audience.

The same applies when looking at galleries. As soon as your work is seen in a particular venue, you and the work are associated with that gallery's standpoint. Ask yourself what you want for your work, how you want it to be seen and what your ambitions are, and this will help you make the right choices. As you, your work and ambitions change, you may want to reassess the context in which you show. Keep this in mind as your career develops.

Success

Talking to artists, I have come to realise that feeling successful doesn't always have a relationship with actual success. Some artists who have achieved a measure of success – or even considerable success – don't recognise themselves as successful or don't enjoy it if they do. For example, an artist who makes a living through a commercial gallery and can work every day in the studio – the dream of many – says he won't be satisfied until he has more recognition. Another is unhappy because she can't make a living from her work, despite having a national reputation and many exhibitions behind her.

It is understandable that ambitious people are never entirely satisfied. The desire for greater achievement is frequently the motivation for continuing work. However, being unable to recognise your own achievements contributes to the impression amongst artists that there isn't enough to go round and to a feeling of powerlessness.

But what is success really like? An artist I spoke to whose work rose to prominence during the '80s told me: "My work disappears before I've had time to even look at it. Buyers are lined up by the gallery before I've begun to work on the paintings they will purchase. My studio is usually empty except for the paintings I am working on. I am constantly under pressure to produce with no time to think." She has also experienced "a lot of jealousy. The artists at my studio won't even take messages for me."

Another explained: "I'm told I'm selfish and that my work means more to me than anything else. But the trouble is, to achieve what you want means you have to focus constantly on your ambitions. Success only comes through hard work and consistent effort. You can't therefore worry too much about what others think." During his show at the Whitechapel Art Gallery Tim Head said: "There are many demands on my time. Since the start of the show I've had dozens of requests from people wanting to interview me, especially students writing theses. I'd like to help them all, but it's just not possible in every case." But in spite of such pressures, artists can appreciate and enjoy their success. Tim Head realises the value of the opportunities open to him, just as Simon Edmondson – who makes a living from his work – acknowledges his good fortune in being able to work in the studio each day.

The main advantage of commercial success is recognised as having time to work, and those who make a living from selling are generally the most content – as long as work doesn't disappear too quickly. Success does not necessarily mean fame and fortune. Many artists develop successful, fulfilling professional lives through a range of related activities including making and exhibiting. Meeting challenges, fulfilling goals and earning respect from colleagues creates well-being that is perhaps the ultimate essence of success.

Making choices

This book demonstrates that artists' careers develop in many different ways and depend on many inter-related factors. What works for one artist may not work for another. It is up to you to decide which path to take and where to go. Early on, it is probably advisable to experiment with what you do, keeping an open mind whilst remaining aware of your personal objectives. Later on, you may need to be selective when opportunities come your way. At other times when you seem stuck, you may need to take the initiative to get things going again. Taking responsibility for your choices enables you to take control of your exhibiting career and increase the likelihood of achieving what you want without closing down the possibility of the unexpected. At the same time, you empower yourself and, by taking this active approach to exhibiting, contribute to the general empowerment of artists.

12 • Further reading

The following books and magazines provide back-up information and further insights into the context for contemporary visual arts practice.

AN Publications

Available from: AN Publications, PO Box 23, Sunderland SR4 6DG. Tel 0191 514 3600.

Art in Public, ed. Susan Jones, 1992, ISBN 0 907730 18 3. Combines coverage of contemporary context for public art with critical examination of projects and practical advice and artists' experiences creating permanent and temporary art, craft and photographic works in public. Price: £9.95 + £1 post.

Artists Newsletter. Monthly visual arts information and analysis. Price: £19.95 UK individual.

Copyright, Roland Miller, 1991, ISBN 0 907730 12 4. Includes advice on copyright and moral rights in exhibitions and promotional material, royalty and licence agreements and copyright abroad. Price: £7.25 + £1 post.

Directory of Exhibition Spaces, 3rd edition, ed. Richard Padwick, 1993, ISBN 0 907730 17 5. Lists over 1600 UK public and private galleries, including museums, libraries, arts centres, universities, theatres and heritage and community exhibition spaces. Price: £13.99 + £1 post.

Exhibiting and Selling Abroad, Judith Staines, 1994, ISBN 0 907730 21 3. For artists, makers and photographers wanting to promote themselves and their work internationally; includes exporting procedures, networking, finding markets, transporting work and sales administration. Price: £7.25 + £1 post.

Fact Pack: Getting Media Coverage, 1993. Advice on attracting the media plus listing of national and regional TV and radio programmes. Price: £1.85 inc post.

Fact Pack: Insurance, 1994. Comprehensive information on artists' insurance needs. Price: £1.85 inc post.

Fact Pack: Mailing the Press, 1993. How to write effective press releases plus listing of national, international and regional press and art media. Price: £1.85 inc post.

Fact Pack: Rates of Pay, 1994. Digest of fees and rates of pay for visual artists for commissions, residencies, workshops and exhibitions plus how to work out hourly rates and cost one-off items. Price: £1.85 inc post.

Fact Pack: Slide Indexes, 2nd edition, 1993. Listing 40 indexes and registers nationally, with details of eligibility and who consults them. Price: £1.85 inc post.

Fundraising: the artist's guide to planning and financing work, ed. Susan Jones, 1993, ISBN 0 907730 20 5. Drawing on artists' experiences and advice, demonstrates how artists and groups can finance exhibitions, travel and other projects through grants from arts boards and trusts, loans and sponsorship. Includes advice on writing applications and budgeting. Price: £7.25 + £1 post.

Introduction to Contracts, Nicholas Sharp, 1993. Outlines elements and terms in legal contracts, with advice on how to negotiate, deal with disputes and find a solicitor. Price: £1.50 inc post.

Licensing Reproductions, Nicholas Sharp, 1994. Explains how to grant or obtain permission to reproduce artwork or designs. Includes sample licence and royalty agreements and advice on types of agreements, fees and royalties, negotiating and monitoring agreements. Price: £3.50 inc post.

Making Ways: the visual artist's guide to surviving and thriving, 3rd edition, ed. David Butler, 1992, ISBN 0 907730 16 7. Covers exhibiting, selling, working in public and with people, collective action, skill sharing, publicity and promotion, studios, health and safety, employment and legal issues, insurance, contracts and copyright with reading and contacts lists. Price: £11.99 + £1 post.

Money Matters, Sarah Deeks, Richard Murphy & Sally Nolan, 1991, ISBN 0 907730 11 6. Artists' financial guide to self-employment covering taxation, VAT, NIC and including accounting system for artists and makers. Price: £7.25 + £1 post.

NAA Public Exhibition Contract, Richard Padwick, 1993. Commissioned by the National Artists Association, covers all aspects of showing work in public galleries and exhibition spaces, including fees, sales arrangements, insurance, promotion and touring. Price: £3.50 inc post.

Organising Your Exhibition – the self-help guide, 2nd edition, Debbie Duffin, ISBN 0 907730 14 0. Covering finding space, costing, time-tabling, publicity, framing, insurance, transporting work, installation, private view, selling and making the best of an exhibition. Price: £7.25 + £1 post.

Selling, Judith Staines, 1993, ISBN 0 907730 19 1. Practical advice based on artists' experiences of promoting and selling art and craft work. Price: £7.25 + £1 post.

Selling Contracts, Nicholas Sharp, 1993. Includes four model contracts, which can be photocopied for personal use, covering direct sales of art and craft work to private buyers, galleries and shops, as well as sale or return agreements. Price: £3.50 inc post.

Art Review

Available from: 20 Prescott Place, London SW4 6BT. Tel 0171 978 1000.

Art Review. Monthly reviews and features on contemporary visual arts. Price: £29.50 UK.

Art Review Yearbook, 22nd edition, 1994, ISBN 0 9044831 14 0. Annual publication including list of UK galleries. Price: £19.50 + £2.50 post.

Arts Council of England

Available from: 14 Great Peter Street, London SW1P 3NQ. Tel 0171 333 0100.

Arts Council Press & Contacts Lists, 1994, ISBN 0 7287 0618 0. Compiled for Arts Council's own use, covers all artforms except crafts, listed by specialisation and region-by-region. Price: £25 inc post.

In Through the Front Door – disabled people and visual arts, Jayne Earnscliffe, 1991, ISBN 0 7287 0649 0. Examples of good practice plus information on access, education, programming and training. Price: £9.95 +£1 post. (Also available

from: AN Publications, PO Box 23, Sunderland SR4 6DG. Tel 0191 514 3600)

Selling the Contemporary Visual Arts, Gerri Morris, 1992. Price: £3.

BBC Publications

Relative Values, Louisa Buck & Philip Dodd, 1991.

Britannia Art Publications

Available from: Suite 17, 26 Charing Cross Road, London WC2H 0DG. Tel 0171 240 0389.

Art Monthly. Published ten times a year, includes features, reviews and exhibition listings. Price: £22.50 UK individual.

British American Arts Association

Available from: 116 Commercial Street, London E1 6NF. Tel 0171 247 5385.

The Artist in the Changing City, Williams, Bollen, Gidney & Owens, 1993, ISBN 0 951476 31 9. Price: £11.45 inc post.

Channel 4 Television

State of the Art, ed. Sandy Nairne, 1987.

CIRCA

Available from: CIRCA Distribution, Mackin Robinson Art Services, 67 Donegall Pass, Belfast BT7 1DR. Tel 0232 237717.

CIRCA. Bi-monthly coverage of visual arts in Ireland. Price: £3.50 per issue.

City University

Available from: City University, Department of Arts Policy & Management, Level 12, Frobisher Crescent, Barbican, Silk Street, London EC2Y 0HB. Tel 0171 477 8887.

Developing the Visual Arts, ed. Eric Moody, 1994. Essays by Nicholas Pearson, Deanna Petherbridge, Eric Moody, Malcolm Miles and Sara Selwood on how visual arts might be developed economically and qualitatively in the 1990s and beyond. Price: £3 + £1 post. (Also available from: AN Publications, PO Box 23, Sunderland SR4 6DG, tel 0191 514 3600.)

Contemporary Art Publishers Ltd

Available from: PO Box 406, Southampton SO14 6ZB. Tel 01703 672006.

Contemporary Art. Quarterly journal with articles and reviews concerned with "presenting art and artists in an accessible way." Price: £3.95 UK per copy.

Crafts Council

Available from: Crafts, 44a Pentonville Road, London N1 9BY.

Crafts. Six issues a year, with features, maker profiles, comment, reviews, business news and gallery listings. Price: £25 UK individual.

Directory of Social Change

Available from: AN Publications, PO Box 23, Sunderland SR4 6DG. Tel 0191 514 3600.

The Arts Funding Guide, 3rd edition, Anne-Marie Doulton, 1994, ISBN 0 907164 27 7. Advice for arts organisations on raising money from arts councils, RABs, local authorities, grant-making trusts and business, plus details of funds from Europe and USA. Price: £15.95 + £1 post plus £1 postage.

Forlaget Scharff

Available from: AN Publications, PO Box 23, Sunderland SR4 6DG. Tel 0191 514 3600.

Directory of International Open Art Exhibitions: Europe, ed. Judith Scharffenberg, 1993, ISBN 87 983852 0 8. Lists over 100 competitions and open exhibitions up and until 1998 for painters, sculptors, printmakers, makers and video artists and includes details of application and acceptance numbers, prices and deadlines. Price: £12 inc post.

Frieze

Available from: 21 Denmark Street, London WC2H 8NE. Tel 0171 379 1533.

Frieze. International visual arts magazine published six times a year. Price: £3.75 UK per copy.

London Art & Artists Guide

London Art and Artists Guide, 6th edition, ed. Heather Waddell, 1993, ISBN 0 952000 40 7. Covers museums, galleries, studios, print publishers, art material suppliers, art magazines, press contacts and prizes and grants plus interviews with dealers and artists. Price: £8.95.

Manchester University Press

New Feminist Art Criticism, ed. Katy Deepwell, 1995, ISBN 0 7190 4258 5. Published February 1995. Price: £14.99.

Nottingham Trent University

Available from: AN Publications, PO Box 23, Sunderland SR4 6DG. Tel 0191 514 3600.

Seeing the Light, ed. Rhonda Wilson, 1993, ISBN 0 905488 19 9. Guide to contemporary survival strategies for independent image makers including festivals, exhibiting and grants, with advice from photographers and galleries. Price: £10 + £1 post.

Second Shift

Available from: 11 Petworth Street, Cambridge CB1 2LY.

Second Shift. Quarterly magazine offering "a wider perspective on women and the arts". Price: £10 UK individual.

Southern Arts Board

Available from: 13 St Clement Street, Winchester, Hampshire SO23 9DQ. Tel 01962 855099.

Guidelines on Exhibiting, 1990. Free to makers in Southern Arts area, due to be updated in 1995.

Publicity & media planning guidelines, 1990. Free to makers in Southern Arts area, due to be updated 1995.

Thames & Hudson

Conditions of Success, Alan Bowness, 1989.

The Art Newspaper

Available from: PO Box 1, Tonbridge, Kent TN9 1HW.

The Art Newspaper. International newspaper published ten times a year, reporting on events, politics and economics in the artworld including diary of international exhibitions and reviews. Price: £30 UK.

Tony Williams Publications

Available from: TW Publications, 24A North Curry, Taunton TA3 6LE.

Craft Galleries, 2nd edition, ed. Caroline Mornement, 1994, ISBN 1 869833 45 7. Covers 55 craft galleries with policies and illustrated profiles of artists they show. Price: £11.50 inc post.

Versus Contemporary Arts

Available from: PO Box HP44, Leeds LS6 2XQ.

Versus. Contemporary art magazine published three times a year providing platform for visual artists, writers and others in the North with issue-based features, short stories, artists' pages and poetry. Price: £11.25 UK.

Women's Art Library

Available from: Women's Art Library, Fulham Palace, Bishops Avenue, London SW6 6EA. Tel 0171 731 7618.

Women's Art Magazine. Bi-monthly journal with discussion, reviews and analysis of work by women artists from the UK, mainland Europe and US. Price: £15 UK individual.

13 • Contacts

This section lists main sources of information and advice on funding for visual arts events including temporary exhibitions and installations.

Arts councils and boards

Arts Council of England, 14 Great Peter Street, London, SW1P 3NQ, tel: 0171 333 0100. Involved with projects and programmes of 'national significance', other funding in England now devolved to regional arts boards.

Arts Council of Northern Ireland, 185 Stranmillis Road, Belfast, BT9 5DU, tel: 01232 381 591.

Arts Council of Wales, Museum Place, Cardiff, CF1 3NX, tel: 01222 394711. Covers visual arts and crafts in Wales.

Crafts Council, 44a Pentonville Road, London, N1 9HF, tel: 0171 278 7700.

Crafts Council of Ireland, The Powers Court, Town House Centre, South William Street, Dublin, 2, Ireland, tel: [010 353] 1 6797368.

East Midlands Arts Board, Mountfields House, Forest Road, Loughborough, LE11 3HU, tel: 0509 218292. Covers Leicestershire, Nottinghamshire, Northamptonshire and Derbyshire except High Peak District.

Eastern Arts Board, Cherry Hinton Hall, Cherry Hinton Road, Cambridge, CB1 4DW, tel: 01223 215355. Covers Bedfordshire, Cambridgeshire, Essex, Hertfordshire, Lincolnshire, Norfolk, Suffolk.

Irish Arts Council, 70 Merrion Square, Dublin, 2, Ireland, tel: [010 353] 1 611840.

North East Wales Office (Arts Council of Wales), Daniel Owen Centre, Earl Road, Mold, Clwyd, CH7 1AP, tel: 01352 758403, fax: 01352 700236.

North Wales Office (Arts Council of Wales), 10 Wellfield House, Bangor, Gwynedd, LL57 1ER, tel: 01248 353248.

North West Arts Board, 4th Floor, 12 Harter Street, Manchester, M1 6HY, tel: 0161 228 3062. Covers Cheshire, Greater Manchester, Lancashire, Merseyside and High Peak District of Derbyshire.

Northern Arts Board, 9/10 Osborne Terrace, Newcastle upon Tyne, NE2 1NZ, tel: 0191 281 6334. Covers Cleveland, Cumbria, Durham, Northumberland and Tyne & Wear.

Scottish Arts Council, 12 Manor Place, Edinburgh, EH3 7DO, tel: 0131 226 6051. Covers visual arts and crafts in Scotland.

South East Arts Board, 10 Mount Ephraim, Tunbridge Wells, TN4 8AS, tel: 01892 515210. Covers Kent, Surrey and East & West Sussex excluding Greater London areas.

South East Wales Office (Arts Council of Wales), Victoria Street, Cwmbran, NP44 3YT, tel: 01633 875075.

South West Arts Board, Bradninch Place, Gandy Street, Exeter, EX4 3LS, tel: 01392 218188. Covers Avon, Cornwall, Devon and Dorset (except Bournemouth, Christchurch and Poole areas), Gloucestershire and Somerset.

Southern Arts Board, 13 St Clement Street, Winchester, SO23 9DQ, tel: 01962 855099, fax: 01962 861186. Covers Berkshire, Buckinghamshire, Hampshire, Isle of Wight, Oxfordshire, Wiltshire, and the Poole, Bournemouth and Christchurch areas of Dorset.

West Midlands Arts Board, 82 Granville Street, Birmingham, B1 2LH, tel: 0121 631 3121. Covers Hereford & Worcester, Shropshire, Staffordshire, Warwickshire and West Midlands.

West Wales Office (Arts Council of Wales), 3 Heol Goch, Carmarthen, Dyfed, SA31 1QL, tel: 01267 234248.

Information

African and Asian Visual Artists Archive, 34 Portland Square, St Paul's, Bristol, BS2 8RQ, tel: 0117 244492. Register and archive for African and Asian artists.

Art Unit/Cytgord Cyf, 8 Rhes Victoria, Bethesda, Gwynedd, LL5 7AG. Produces *Art Unit Magazine* and *Art Bulletin* for visual arts sector in Wales.

Arts for Health, Manchester Metropolitan University, All Saints, Manchester, M15 6BY, tel: 0161 236 8916. Advice and information on health care arts.

AXIS – visual arts information service, Leeds Metropolitan University, Calverley Street, Leeds, LS1 3HE, tel: 0113 283 3125, fax 0113 283 3112, contact: Yvonne Deane.

CAFE (Creative Activity for Everyone), 23/25 Moss Street, Dublin, 2, tel: [010 353] 677 0330. Holds lists of creative people organisations, resources and exhibition spaces across Ireland.

Panchayat, Unit 23, Spitalfields Art Project, 11-18 Steward Street, London, E1 6AL, tel: 0171 377 5958. Information on South Asian artists.

Professional associations

Art & Architecture Ltd, c/o Peter Rawsthorne, Rawsthorne Associates, 'Dunsdale', Forest Row, E Sussex, RH18 5BD, tel: 0134 282 2704, contact: Peter Rawsthorne.

Association of Artists in Ireland (AAI), Room 803 Liberty Hall, Dublin 1, Ireland, tel: [010 353] 1 740529, fax: [010 353] 1 740529.

Design & Artists Copyright Society Ltd (DACS), St Mary's Clergy House, 2 Whitechurch Lane, London, E1 7QR, tel: 0171 247 1650.

National Artists Association (NAA), Interchange Studios, Dalby Street, London NW5 3NQ, tel: 0171 267 0420.

National Association for Gallery Education, 8 de Montfort Road, Lewes, BN7 1SP, tel: 01273 478692.

Public Art Forum, Flat 1, The Priory, Webber Street, London, SE1 0RQ, tel: 0171 928 1221, contact: Lisa Harty.

Visual Arts and Galleries Association, The Old School, Witcham, Ely, CB6 2LQ, tel: 01353 776356, contact: Hilary Gresty.

Public art agencies

Art in Partnership, 233 Cowgate, Edinburgh, EH1 1NQ, tel: 0131 225 4463, contact: Robert Breen.

Artangel Trust, 133 Oxford Street, London, W1R 1TD, tel: 0171 434 2887, contact: Michael Morris/ James Lingwood.

Artists' Agency, 18 Norfolk Street, Sunderland, SR1 1EA, tel: 0191 510 9318, contact: Lucy Miton/ Esther Salamon.

Cardiff Bay Arts Trust, Pilotage House, Stuart Street, Cardiff, CF1 6BW, tel: 01222 488772.

Artpoint, Great Barn, Parklands, Great Linford, Milton Keynes, MK14 5DZ, tel: 01908 606791.

Commissions East, 6 Kings Parade, Cambridge, CB2 1SJ, tel: 01223 356882.

Cywaith Cymru/Artworks Wales, 2 John Street, Cardiff, CF1 5AE, tel: 01222 489543.

Health Care Arts (England & Wales), 10 Clarendon Road, Leeds.

Health Care Arts (Scotland & Ireland), 23 Springfield, Dundee, DD1 4JE, tel: 01382 203099, contact: Elizabeth McFall.

Independent Public Arts, 25 Greenside Place, Edinburgh, EH1 3AA, tel: 0151 558 1950, contact: Jonathon Colin/Juliet Dean.

Public Art Commissions Agency, Studio 6, Victoria Works, Vittoria Street, Birmingham, B1 3PE, tel: 0121 212 4454, contact: Vivien Lovell.

Public Art Development Trust, 3rd Floor, Kirkman House, 12-14 Whitfield Street, London, W1P 5RD, tel: 0171 580 9977, fax: 0171 580 8540, contact: Sandra Percival.

Public Art Swindon, Thamesdown Borough Council, Euclid Street, Swindon, SN1 2JH , tel: 01793 493196.

Public Arts, 24 Bond Street, Wakefield, WF1 2QP, tel: 01924 295791, contact: Graham Roberts.

Index

Page numbers in italics refer to illustrations.
Numbers in bold refer to illustrative examples.

A

Aberdeen: installation project 53; Royal Infirmary, gallery *13*
Adam Gallery, London 39, **41**, 43
administrators 10
Aerial project 52
African and Asian Visual Artists Archive 111
age, of exhibitors 9, 22
agents and agencies 9; at open exhibitions 56; dealers used as agents by collectors 15; employed by businesses 11; organising exhibitions 49, 52-3
Anderson, Wendy, artist 46
Andrew Lamont Gallery, London 27
Angela Flowers Gallery, London 30
Anne Berthoud Gallery 52
Antwerp, Galerie Ruimte Morguen *86*
applications: documentation 79-81, 83-5; for exhibition spaces (non-galleries) 45-6; importance of research 38, 45, 46, 69-70; to commercial galleries 30-1; to hire galleries 47; to subsidised galleries 37-8; unsolicited 30, 37
art classes 64
art education, and women 21
art fairs 32
art market 10, 14-15, 19
Art Monthly 13, 14
Art for Offices **11**, 28
art press (magazines) 13, 14, 17, 23, 55
Artangel Trust 49, **50**
artist-run galleries and spaces 39-43, 71
artists: acting as independent curators 10, 58; affinities and allegiances 16; agendas and motivations 16-17, 66; assessing your work 95; attitudes and definitions 8-9; being assertive 74, 102; being professional 74-5; broadening audiences 90, 96-8; building up relationships 53, 76-7; changes in work or style and the attitudes of galleries 31-2; communication skills 69, **75**; coping with isolation 72, **74**; coping with success 104-5; dealing with rejections 76, 87; discrimination against older artists 22; evaluating the experience of an exhibition 100-6; exclusive arrangements with a gallery 29-30; gaining confidence 53, 70, 74, 75, 78-9; handling interviews 85; handling studio visits 85-6; if approached by a gallery 84-5; making and developing contacts 75-6; making a plan of action 72-7; organising and financing a show 46, 47-8, 49-53; and private and public collectors 11-13; relationship with subsidised galleries 39; selected by independent curators 59-60; selection, criteria used by galleries 66; as stars 9-10; starting work again after a show 101; talking about your work 70, 86-7; what to do after the show is over (contacts, follow-ups) 90-2, 98-9, 100-6; what to do if things go wrong 92-3; as writers 76; writing about your work 75, 81; *see also* black artists; sales; self-assessment
Artists Newsletter 55, 74, 98
arts boards *see* regional arts boards
arts centres 32, 71
Arts Council of England 34; address 110; increased funding to the regions 23; Live Art Travel and Research 59; policy of cultural diversity 21; purchases for its collection 12
arts councils 74; addresses 110; funding by 32, 59
arts festivals 23, 49, 74
Asian artists: information for 111; women 97
Atherton, Kevin, artist 9
auction houses 10, 15, 19
AXIS 111

B

Babrah, Ranbir, artist 97
Baumgarten, Lothar, installation artist *23*
Belfast, Flax Art Studios 53
Bell, Frederick, artist *86*
Bermondsey Artists Group 40
Bickers, Patricia, magazine editor 14
black artists 21
Boddington, Sophie, artist *82*
Bonaventura, Paul 34
British Council 12

businesses: commissions for 11, 72; corporate collections of art 11; selection of work 11; as sponsors 17, 19, 35, 39, 49, 50

C

Cadwallader, Helen, curator 59
Café Gallery, Southwark Park 21, 39, **40**, 40-1, 43, 55; education programme 40, 64
cafés, exhibition spaces in 43, 44, 71
Callery, Simon, artist 64, 65
Camden Arts Centre 63, 64
Camerawork 19
Castlefield Gallery, Manchester 23, 41, **42**
catalogues 32, 90; include with an application 79; providing photographs for 83; as useful promotional material 14, 56
Central Space, London 19, 36, **37**, 75
ceramics 12, 28
Chantry House Gallery, West Yorkshire 28
charitable trusts, funding from 32, 34, 35
Cleveland Crafts Centre, Middlesbrough *12*
Colchester *see* Printworks
collaborations, on temporary presentations 50
Collective Gallery, Edinburgh 23
collectors 11-13, 15, 20
commercial galleries 17, 19, 25-32; advantages and disadvantages 31-2; audiences 28-9; and collectors 15; exhibition programmes 27-8; handling promotional work after the show 91; making a choice 71; organisers/directors of 10; owners of 27; relationship with artist 29-30, 101; responsibility of 88, 91; sales commission 61, 88; selection and applications 30-1
commission: paid to some hire galleries 48; on sales 13, 61-2, 88
Commonwealth Institute Gallery 22, **36**
Contemporary Applied Arts 28
Contemporary Art 13
Contemporary Art Society 12, 47
Contemporary Ceramics 28
contracts or written agreements 62, 85, 88, 92, 93; exclusive 29, 101-2
Cooper, Linda, artist *101*
Coppock, Chris, gallery director 36
courses: in arts administration 36; to develop skills 72, 74, 75; to gain skills in educational settings 98
Coventry University Gallery 43, 44, 45, 46, 58; audience 44
covering letter 79, 83
craft (and design) galleries 28, 32, 38; sales commission 61
crafts (and craftspeople) 13, 28, 97
Crafts Council 79; address 110; collection on interactive picture bank 12; London shop 28
Crafts (magazine) 13
Craftspace Touring 97
critics 13, 16, 18, 32, 63, 71; as curators 10, 58

Crypt Gallery, St George's Church, London 48
Cubitt Studios, London 41, **42**
cultural diversity 21-2, 97
curators (independent) 8, 10, 58-60, 71, 76; advantages and disadvantages 60; for artist-run exhibitions 41; at open exhibitions 56; finding artists for exhibitions 59-60; relationship with artist 77
curriculum vitae (CV) 79, 80-1

D

dealers 10, 15, 17, 31
Directory of Exhibition Spaces 70
documentation: for an application 75, 79-81, 83-4, 85; of the exhibition 94

E

East End Open Studios 50
Eastbourne Biennial 57
Edinburgh: Aerial project 52; Centre for Collective Art 38
Edmondson, Simon, artist 9, 32, 62, 95, 105
educational activities 19, 32, 34, 39, 63-5, 71, 98, 101; professional associations, addresses 111
educational institutions, funding from 32
educationalists, at open exhibitions 56
Elbow Room Gallery 21
evaluating the experience of shows 100-6; continuing gallery relationships 101-2; deciding what comes next 102-3; developing a context for your work 103-4; success and achievements 104-5
exhibition organisers *see* organisers
Exhibition Payment Right (EPR) 38
exhibition spaces (other than in galleries) 20, 25, 43-7; advantages and disadvantages 46-7; audiences 44; financing 43-4; organisers 43; programming 44-5; selection of work 45-6
exhibitions, making them work 88-99; after the show is over 98-9; approaching other galleries 91; assessing your work 95; broadening audiences to include educational activities 96-8; documenting the show 94; if things go wrong 92-3; pursuing exhibitions 90-1; *see also* publicity and promotion; sales

F

fine art galleries, sales commission 61
Fine Rats International 49
Flotsam-Jetsam 50, **51**
Food Giant (supermarket) 51
France, John, artist and lecturer 58, 59
Freud's Café, exhibition space 43-4, 45
Friar, David, artist *52*
funding: for artist-run spaces 41, 46; by local authorities 12, 19, 32, 33, 34, 43; of exhibition spaces 43-4; for independently-curated exhibitions 58-9, 60; of temporary presentations

Index

(open studios, etc.) 49, 53; *see also* businesses; grants; sponsorship

G

galleries: agenda of and allegiances 16, 66; application forms 83; approaches to 66, 67, 78-87; and the artist 9; artists receive a fee (EPR) 38; artists taking the initiative to organise educational work 98; assessing the professionalism of artists 75; for black artists and curators 21; building up relationships with artists 76-7; changes and developments 18-19; covering letter to 83; for craftspeople and designer-artists 28; and curators 10; and dealers 10; employed by businesses 11; exclusive arangements with an artist 29-30; hierarchies 17, 18; if a gallery makes an approach to an artist 84-5; interviews and studio visits 85-7; making a first telephone call to 78-9; printed publicity material 90; and private collectors 11; publicity and promotion 89; researching and assessing before approaching 70; and sales of work 61-2, 93-4; selecting artists 66; and women 20; workshops 98; and young and older artists 22; *see also* applications
gallerists 10
gallery directors 10, 11, 17, 19, 61, 78, 90, 91, 93; agenda or motivating factor of 16; and artists' professionalism 75; at open studio events 50; in the commerical sector 25; and exhibition programmes 28; interviews with 85; invited to exhibitions 76; studio visits by 85-6; of subsidised galleries 25, 35-7
Gardiner, Dan, artist 55
Gateshead Libraries and Arts 63
Geesin, Dan, installation artist *44*
Gimpel Fils 9, 27, **29**
Glasgow *see* Transmission Gallery
Godfrey & Twatt, Harrogate 28, *79*
Graham-Dixon, Francis, gallery owner 27, 29, 30-1, 76-7
Grampian Hospitals Art Project 13
grants 25, 35
group shows 27-8, 90, 92, 101
Guardian: reviews in 55; specialist arts guides for the regions 23
Guildhall Gallery, Winchester 33
Gupta, Sunil, artist-curator 59

H

Hamlyn, Jane, ceramic artist 28
Harrogate *see* Godfrey & Twatt
Havers, Mandy, sculptor *31*
Hayles Café gallery 43, 45, 74
Haymarket Theatre, Leicester 43, 44; audience 44; programmes 45
Head, Tim, artist 34, 105
healthcare settings: for art 12-13, 34; Arts for Health 111; Health Care Arts 111

Hedge, Paul, gallery organiser 43, 44, 45-6, 74
Henocq, Ron, gallery director 21, 39, 40
hierarchies, in the art world 17-18
Higherwater gallery, London 27
Himid, Lubiana, artist 6, 21
hire galleries 19, 47-8
Holland, Tracey, photographer *22*
hospitals, exhibiting space in 13

I

installations 10, 37, 38, 39, 44, 45, 49, 53, 64, 71; visual documentation of 83-4
Institute of New International Visual Arts (INIVA) 21, 59
Interim Art 18-19, 30
invitations, to a gallery 90
Ireland 13, 53; Crafts Council 110; information 111; Irish Arts Council 110
Irvin, Albert, artist 9
Isis Gallery, Cumbria 101
Isle of Skye 26

I

John Moores Liverpool Exhibition 54, **56**

K

K Foundation 15
Kent, Sarah, magazine editor 14
Kivland, Sharon 19

L

Lake, Suzy, gallery secretary 48
Lambert, Alison, painter 32
Lampert, Catherine, gallery director 34
Lancaster, John, artist *73*
lectures 53, 63, 66, 96-7
Leeds Metropolitan University 37
Lehtonen, Timo, artist *45*
libraries: exhibition space in 33, 43, 44-5, 71, 88; gallery staff 36-7; hierarchy of 18; picture loan schemes 12; selection of work 45; visitor numbers 44
Lisson Gallery 28
Lloyd, Alison, exhibition organiser 36
Local Arts Development Agencies (LADAs) 51, 52
local authorities: funding affected by cutbacks 12, 19, 61; funding from 32, 33, 34, 37, 43, 49, 51; gallery keepers 36; museum collections 12; percent for art 23
local radio 13, 50
Locus + 53
Logsdale, Nicholas, gallery director 28
London 23-4, 29; Arts Board 37, 40; Cork Street 26, 55; Docklands, empty spaces used for exhibiting 20; galleries *see by name;* Museum of Women's Art 20; Tobacco Dock used as exhibition space 51
Long and Ryle gallery, London 32

M

Macgregor, Elizabeth, gallery director 20
magazines: advertising in 89; and dealers 17;
editorial decisions about what to feature 13, 14;
research into 70; writers for 14
Maidstone Library Gallery, workshops 64
mailing lists 41, 76
Manchester: Central Library 44-5; City Art Galleries,
artistic policy 33, see also Castlefield Gallery
Manchester Artists Studio Association 42
media coverage 9, **13-14**, 15, 16, 20, 39, 66, 85, 89,
90; artists contribution to interviews 88; for
independently-curated exhibitions 60; of open
exhibitions 56; of open studio events 50;
providing visual material for 83, 94
Middlesbrough: Art Gallery 36; Cleveland Crafts
Centre *12*
mixed shows 27, 30, 34, 37, 43, 90, 92
Mumbles Gallery, Swansea 26
municipal art galleries 32
Museum of London: audience 44; gallery exhibitions
44; programmes 45; residency at 45; selection
46
Museum of Women's Art 20
museums 10, 11-12, 15, 17

N

Nandia, Indira, gallery director 22, 36, 38
Nelson, Steve, artist 63-4
networking 16, 59
Newcastle upon Tyne: All Saints Church, installation
53; University, Long gallery 37
newspapers, local and national 13, 18, 50
Nicholas Treadwell Gallery 31
Northern Arts Board 51; address 110; exhibitions,
events and commissions scheme **35**; funding
policy 33, 35
Northern Ireland, Arts Council 110
Norwich Gallery, 'East' exhibition 54-5, **56**
Nottingham, Angel Row Gallery *86*

O

Old Fire Station Arts Centre, Oxford 47
open exhibitions 54-7; advantages and
disadvantages 56-7; advertising for 55
open studio shows and events 21, 23, 32, 40, 49,
50, 52, 71, 74
Orbost Gallery, Isle of Skye *26*
organisers 8, 10, 43; at open studio events 50; of
hire galleries 48; of subsidised spaces 35-7
Oxford, arts centre 47

P

Paley, Maureen, gallery director 19, 30, 76
Parker, Cornelia, artist 9, 60, 72, *77*
Peake, Laurie, education officer 63, 65
Pepperall, Anna, gallery organiser 63, 65
percent for art policies 23

performance art 39
Phipps, Anna 29
photographs: with an application 78, 83, 84, 85;
provided for the media 83, 94
photography and photographers 19, 22, 28, 59, 86;
galleries 32
picture loan schemes 12
Povall, Steve, printmaker *30*
press releases 14
previews 39
printmakers 30
Printworks, Colchester 30, 31
private collectors 11
private galleries 17, 26, 54; handling promotional
work after the show 91; if things go wrong 93
private views 88, 90-1, **92**, 94; and sales 93
professional associations, addresses 111
public art agencies, addresses 111
public collections 11-13
public funds (subsidies) 17, 19, 32, 33, 35, 49
public galleries 15
publicity and promotion 29, 44, 70, **89-90**; for artist-
run galleries 41, 43; by exhibitors in hired
spaces 46, 48; by subsidised galleries 17, 38;
for independently-curated exhibitions 60; who is
responsible for 88

R

Raftery, Alison 77
Rama, Samena, photographer 59
Ranjit Kaur Dhanjai, artist *97*
regional arts boards 23, 74; funding from 32, 33, 59;
using resources of 74
regional galleries 24
Remery, Jackie, hire-gallery manager 47, 48
researchers, for television 14
residencies 15, 63-4, 65, 96; at the Museum of
London 45; in schools 63-4; for women 21
reviews 13, 14, 18, 66, 70, 89; having prints
available for 94; include copies of with an
application 79
Reynolds, Adam, gallery director 39, 41
Roberts, Kay, curator 58, 59, 77
Robinson, Elly, gallery director 31
Robinson Road Studios, London 49, 52
Royal Academy 18, 22; Summer Show 55

S

sales 69, 93-4; at auction 15; commission on 61-2;
earning a living (or not) from 9, 32, 62; from hire
galleries 48; from open studio events 52; pricing
work consistently 61; from subsidised galleries
38-9; in libraries, theatres, cafes etc 44
schools 63, 71; galleries in 33; residencies in 63-4
Scotland 38; galleries 23, 26; interactive computer
system 12; public art agencies 111
Scottish Arts Council 12, 110
Sebestyen, Amanda, independent curator 58, 59-60

Index

self-assessment 66-77; action plan 72-7; creating opportunities 71-2; making an informed choice 70-1; realistic expectations 69; research and researching galleries 69-70; strategy for applications to galleries, and questions to ask yourself 67-9; time-scales and relationships 76-7

Sellars, Peter, artist and film-maker 8
seminars 97, 104
'Signals: Festival of Women Photographers' 22
Silver, Susanne, artist 53
slides: as an application (selection of work from) 31, 33, 37, 38, 40, 48, 56, 72, 78, 79, **83**, **84**; of the exhibition 94; for lectures 96-7
Slidex, index of artists 42
Smith, Duncan, artist and gallery director 36, 37, 75
Smith, Helen, artist 51, 52
Smith, Terry, artist 51
Smiths Gallery, London 47, 48
solo shows 28, 33, 37, 41, 44, 90, 92; as a prize 57
South Asian artists 111
South Asian Arts 97
South West Arts Board 73, 110
Spain, Simon, artist 50, 51
special needs school groups 64
sponsors and sponsorship 17, 25, 34, 35, 39, 49, 50, 54, 55, 61
Staffordshire University, Women's Photography Project 22
Stevens, Samantha, manager 43
Stockham, Jo, installation artist 64
Strictly Textiles group 64
students 76
studio groups, galleries established by 39
studio visits by gallery directors 85-6
studios see open studio shows and events
subsidised galleries 17, 19, 25, 32-9, 71, 91; advantages and disadvantages 38-9; approaches to 78; artist's relationship with 101; directors or organisers 35-7; and educational activities 32, 39, 63, 96; funding criteria 33, 35, 61; selection and applications 37-8; and women artists 20
Sunderland City Council Arts Unit 51
supermarket, as art space 51
Swansea 26

T

talks and guided tours 96, 97
telephone techniques, to a gallery 78-9
television coverage 14
temporary presentations 49-53; advantages and disadvantages 51-3; audience response 49-50; collaborations 50; see also open studio shows and events
theatres, exhibition spaces 43, and see also Haymarket Theatre
Thumb Gallery, London 30
time-based work 39; visual documentation of 83-4
Tong, Kim, artist 104
touring exhibitions 14, 58, 97; buying from 38-9
Transmission Gallery, Glasgow 23
Treuherz, Julian, gallery keeper 56

U

Uckfield, East Sussex 44
universities: exhibition spaces in 33, 43, 44, 58; gallery staff 37
Usher Gallery, Lincoln 104

V

Victoria and Albert Museum, London, purchase fund 12

W

Wales: arts councils and boards 110; information 111; public art agencies 111
Whitechapel Art Gallery, London 34, 64, 105
Whitechapel Open exhibition **34**, 50, **54**, 95
Whiteread, Rachel, artist 15, 49
Whitworth Young Contemporaries 55
Winchester see Guildhall Gallery
women: artists and gallery directors 20-1, 22; Asian 97
workshops 63, 65, 66, 96, **98**, 104; textiles 64; to help increase presentation skills 69
Worley, Sara, textile artist 64
writers 13-14, 18, 70; as independent curators 10, 58; invited to exhibitions 76

Y

Year of the Visual Arts (Visual Arts Region 1996) 35

PUBLICATIONS

Artists Handbooks

If you've found this book useful, why not check out the rest of the series? This steadily growing and well-respected portfolio of books deals with important aspects of visual arts practice now. Combining practical suggestions drawn from artists' own experiences with sound research and facts, these books are a unique resource, not only for visual artists at all stages of their careers and those studying art and design, but for arts organisers and officers, educationalists, careers and business advisers and all others involved with the arts.

Exhibiting & Selling Abroad

Judith Staines

Invaluable handbook for artists, makers and photographers who want to promote themselves and their work internationally, investigating everything from exhibitions and trade fairs to residencies and studio visits. With chapters on the practicalities of exporting work for sale, finding markets, sales administration and networking, *Exhibiting & Selling Abroad* also has plenty of examples of artists' and makers' own experiences.

PB, A5, 120pp, illus, ISBN 0 907730 21 3, £7.25

Fundraising

The artist's guide to planning and financing work

Ed. Susan Jones

Drawing on artists' first-hand experiences and advice, this book demonstrates the many ways in which artists and groups can finance exhibitions, travel, workspace, exploration and projects, ranging from grants from arts boards and charitable trusts to loans linked with business advice and from patronage to subsidised workspace. Showing how artists can mix and match sources, using one to lever another or combining several to realise large-scale projects, it is invaluable to artists, students, arts organisers and all others initiating and developing visual arts projects.

PB, A5, 134pp, illus, ISBN 0 90 7730 20 5, £7.25

Funded by THE ARTS COUNCIL OF ENGLAND

PUBLICATIONS

Selling

Judith Staines

This much-needed book is for visual artists, crafts-people and photographers who want to sell their work. It doesn't explain how to get rich quick or teach slippery sales techniques, but does offer a realistic, supportive and practical approach to the business of selling. Using examples of how artists have promoted themselves and found markets for their work, *Selling* covers where and how to sell, pricing work and the fundamentals of administration and getting paid.

Whether you make decorative weavings, do abstract paintings on ceramics, create portraits or ephemeral installations, by adopting a proactive approach to selling and adding perseverance, imagination and a degree of good luck, it can be a profitable activity.

PB, A5, 136pp, illus, ISBN 0 907730 19 1, £7.25

Making Ways

The visual artist's guide to surviving and thriving

Ed. David Butler

Described by many artists as the most useful book they've ever bought, *Making Ways* covers everything from exhibiting to working in the community, from promotion to setting up a studio and from benefits to public art.

PB, A5, 256pp, illus, ISBN 0 907730 16 7, £11.99

Directory of Exhibition Spaces

Ed. Richard Padwick

3rd Edition

A comprehensive guide to over 1600 galleries and exhibition spaces in England, Scotland, Northern Ireland and Wales, this is the third edition of an invaluable reference book for artists, makers and photographers seeking places to show and sell work, gallery organisers looking to exchange or tour exhibitions as well as for those wishing to find out where to see fine art, craft and photographic work.

PB, A5, 259pp, ISBN 0 907730 17 5, £13.99

Art in Public

What, why and how

Ed. Susan Jones

Essential reading for everyone interested or involved in art in public places, this timely book combines coverage of the contemporary context for public art with critical examination of projects and practical advice. By describing artists' experiences of permanent and temporary art, craft and photographic works in public locations, it is a valuable resource for artists wishing to initiate their own projects and work on an equal footing with other professionals.

PB, A5, 178pp, illus, ISBN 0 907730 18 3, £9.95

PUBLICATIONS

Live Art

Ed. Robert Ayers & David Butler

If your work involves live or temporary elements, this book is essential reading. Including advice on how to develop and manage a performance, touring, copyright, contracts and documentation and with numerous examples of artists' own experiences, *Live Art* is a must for all who want to perform, curate or promote live art.

PB, A5, 178pp, illus, ISBN 0 907730 13 2, £7.25

Money Matters

The artist's financial guide

Sarah Deeks, Richard Murphy & Sally Nolan

Reliable, user-friendly advice on taxation, National Insurance, VAT, keeping accounts, pricing, grants and dealing with suppliers, customers and banks. Features an excellent accounting system for all visual artists.

PB, A5, 134pp, illus, ISBN 0 907730 11 6, £7.25

Organising Your Exhibition

The self-help guide

Debbie Duffin

Frustrated by applying and being rejected by galleries? Here's a book which shows how to take control and organise your own exhibition. Covers finding and using alternative spaces plus costing, schedules, installation, publicity, selling and educational activities.

PB, A5, 116pp, illus, ISBN 0 907730 14 0, £7.25

Across Europe

The artist's personal guide to travel & work

Ed. David Butler

Immensely readable handbook looking at 24 European countries through the eyes of indigenous and UK artists and providing an insight into potential opportunities for travelling, working or studying abroad. Covering funding, exhibiting, how to make contacts, education and selling and with an extensive information section, *Across Europe* is a must for artists, galleries and arts organisers.

PB, A5, 168pp, illus, ISBN 0 907730 15 9, £9.95. Comes with a free copy of the *Artists and the EU* Fact Pack

Copyright

Protection, use and responsibilities

Roland Miller

Designed to answer all copyright problems, this book contains essential advice on negotiating copyright agreements, exploiting the earning and promotional potential of copyright and dealing with infringement and includes down-to-earth discussion of what happens in real life when artists' images are used.

PB, A5, 125pp, illus, ISBN 0 907730 12 4, £7.25

PUBLICATIONS

Visual Arts Contracts

A response to the growing desire amongst artists and administrators to use sound legal agreements, our Visual Arts Contracts are ready to use and written in straightforward language. Each covers a specialist area, either as easy-to-complete forms or as a point-by-point checklist with explanatory notes. Written by solicitor Nicholas Sharp, these contracts will ensure effective collaborations between artists, exhibition organisers, agents and commissioners. Price includes postage.

Commission Contracts

Probably the most complex and demanding of all contractual areas for visual artists, this sets the legal scene for commissioning and public art processes.
By comparing public and private arrangements and describing the roles of parties in public art commissions, functions of agents and dealers and the implications of sub-contracting, it is an essential guide to good practice in an area which can be a minefield for artists. Also contains information on fees, ownership and copyright, moral rights, insurance and termination, with fill-in contract forms covering Commissioned Design, Commission and Sale for Public Art, and Private Commission Contracts.
PB, A4, 20 pp, £3.50

Introduction to Contracts

Outlines elements and terms in contracts, providing advice on how to negotiate, deal with disputes and find a solicitor.
PB, A4, 12pp, £1.50

Selling Contracts

Specifically concerned with selling art and craft work, this covers selling to private buyers, galleries and shops as well as contracts for sale or return.
PB, A4, 14pp, £3.50

NAA Public Exhibition Contract

Commissioned from Richard Padwick by the National Artists Association – the representative body for visual artists – this covers showing work in public galleries and exhibition spaces and includes fees, sales arrangements, insurance, promotion, touring.
PB, A4, 24pp, £3.50

Licensing Reproductions

Explains in straightforward terms how to grant or obtain permission to reproduce artwork or designs including what licensing agreements to use, fees and royalties, negotiating and monitoring agreements.
PB, A4, 20pp, £3.50

Ordering details

For mail orders add £1 per order for postage (UK) £2 per order (Europe) £4 per order (Overseas).
Telephone creditcard orders to 091 514 3600, or write to: PO Box 23, Sunderland, SR4 6DG (prices quoted at November '94 are subject to change)